Grueling labor for St. Martin children, loading salt from the Great Salt Pond onto a lighter on Great Bay Beach. The load of salt would be transferred in the small boat to the ship anchored in Great Bay Harbor. Philipsburg, 1923. (Source: *Het zoutbedrijf op St. Martin*)

BOOKS BY HOUSE OF NEHESI PUBLISHERS

Nomad
Yvonne Weekes

Liviticus
Kamau Brathwaite

Columbus, The Moor | Colón, el Moro
Colomb, le Maure | Colombo, il Moro
Charles Matz

The Adulterous Citizen
poems stories essays
Tishani Doshi

Haïti et l'identité littéraire trans-caribéenne
Emilio Jorge Rodríguez

Book of Sins
Nidaa Khoury

Guanahani, My Love
Marion Bethel

Coming, Coming Home
Western Education and the Caribbean Intellectual
George Lamming

Eva/Sión/Es • Eva/Sion/s • Éva/Sion/s
Chiqui Vicioso

The Angel Horn
Shake Keane (1927-1997) Collected Poems
Shake Keane

The Essence Reparation
Amiri Baraka

Friendly Anger
The Rise of the Labor Movement in St. Martin
Joseph H. Lake, Jr.

number of noted writers, including Tip Marugg and Frank Martinus Arion (Curacao), Will Johnson (Saba), and others. However, some literary historians claim that few, if any, of the writers from this area of the Caribbean have so far made it to what they consider the center-stage of the region's literature. From reading Dr. Florian's book, I incline to the view that the work of Lasana M. Sekou could contribute significantly to changing this perception.

There are conflicting attitudes to salt. Jesus of Nazareth reportedly called his followers "the salt of the earth." When you succeed, you are said to be "worth your salt." I read somewhere that Africans traded their gold for salt from the Arabs. The body needs salt to function, but it can manage very well without gold! I was reminded of this when, on a visit to my home district in Jamaica, the first thing an elderly man said to me was, "You bring any salt-ting?" He was hoping that I had brought him gifts of salt-fish, red herring, or salted pork that he could use to flavor the less savory ground provisions such as yam, cassava, and boiled green bananas that were an important part of his diet. The forced crossing of the salty ocean via the Middle Passage into Slavery seems to have altered the attitudes of some diaspora Africans to salt. It is said that some believed that if they ate salt, their souls would be unable to return to Africa. The brethren and sistren of Ras Tafari omit salt from their diet. In Jamaica, when things go badly with you, it is said that you are "salt." As a student

FOREWORD

Sugar and salt are controversial nutritional substances. They are less controversial in Caribbean thought since it is well-known that both have played major roles in the history, economics, society, and culture of the region. This book is about the latter.

For nearly 200 years of colonialism and Slavery, staring around the mid-1600s, salt was the most important part of the economy of St. Martin, a 37-square-mile Caribbean island—its southern half is today yet a territory of the Netherlands, and the northern part is a territory of France. Here, and especially given the historical record of the volume of salt reaped in the Great Salt Pond, which is located in the "Netherlands part," salt seems to have had the edge over sugar, its great rival and accomplice in the colonization and subordination of the peoples of the *Antilles*, my favorite name for the region.

Lasana M. Sekou, one of its leading writers, has chosen salt as one of the main metaphors employed in his work. Dr. Sara Florian, an emerging Caribbeanist with a strong interest in the literature of this region, and especially its poetry, has written an engaging, illuminating, and important study of Sekou's use of the metaphor of salt in his poetry, as well as in his fiction and non-fiction. The "Dutch" territories of this region have produced a

Contents

Foreword	*ix*
Introducing The Poet and His "I-land"	*xvii*
An Aesthetics of Salt and Sugar	**1**
On salt and sugar	4
The salt pyramids of St. Martin	20
Early grains: symbols of the woman, the land, the salt	39
Salty lives of some island women	44
The Creole Abeng: *Marronage* in Sekou's Poetry	**54**
St. Martin: colonial or postcolonial?	66
"Resistance Nation" and a theory of the "village chiefs"	72
Maroons' call-up	82
Languages of Sekouism	84
Sekou's solo and choral voice	108
Evolution of a "West Indian" Aesthetics	**111**
Aesthetic flourishes and solos in a Caribbean poetic ensemble	111
Sekou's Socio-Aesthetic Fabric in a Caribbean Fine-grained Poetic Panoply	**129**
Appendix	*134*
Endnotes	*145*
Bibliography	*158*
About the Author	*176*

"vos estis sal terrae."*

**"you are the salt of the earth." (5:13, Vulgate)*

HOUSE OF NEHESI PUBLISHERS
P.O. Box 460
Philipsburg, St. Martin
Caribbean

WWW.HOUSEOFNEHESIPUBLISH.COM
http://twitter.com/#!/HouseofNehesi
www.facebook.com/HNPbooksauthors

St. Martin Book Fair Edition © 2019 Sara Florian.
All rights reserved.
ISBN: 9780997489569
LC Control Number: 2018931090

Author's acknowledgement: I would like to thank
my family and Lasana, both for providing constant inspiration.

Disclaimer note: although the author and publisher have
made the efforts to trace copyright holders, if any has been
inadvertently overlooked, they are ready to make the
necessary corrections as soon as possible.

Cover design by Sundiata Lake.
Cover art, original portrait on wood by Fay Helfer.
© Private collection. Author's photograph, courtesy S. Florian.

Caribbean Counterpoint

The Aesthetics of Salt in Lasana Sekou

SARA FLORIAN, PHD

in the USA, I had a summer job assisting a professor with a research project, and my task was to spend long hours collating and stapling the questionnaires. One day he stopped to observe me at my labor and said, "It is like working in the salt mines, isn't it?" At the time I did not know anything about salt mines and that people labored in them. Thanks to the writings of Sekou and Dr. Florian's book on it, I now know about the links between salt mines and Slavery in St. Martin, and why literary treatment of this experience can add to our understanding of the Caribbean.

In *Caribbean Counterpoint: The Aesthetics of Salt in Lasana Sekou*, Dr. Florian is clearly interested in showing the significance of this author's work for the Caribbean. She also intends to use the musical phenomenon known as Counterpoint as an important symbol. The term "aesthetics" is from academic philosophy, and it embraces philosophy of literature, the branch of it that is most applicable here. She intends to bring all of this to bear on the literary uses of salt that can be found in the work of Sekou. The book, therefore, intends to include the importance of the symbolism of salt in the quest for meaning in the Caribbean, the musicality of salt, and the aesthetics of salt as part of this quest, especially as they are revealed in the work of this author.

Dr. Florian alludes to Kamau Brathwaite's designation of the "submarine"—below-the-salt-water-unity of the

Caribbean. She wants to make the case that Sekou's concern with salt reflects this. She explores how this can be seen in the content of his writing. I think there is another dimension to this. Historians have observed that in spite of their legendary efficiency, and some add their notorious cruelty, the Dutch made less of an impact on the Caribbean than their British, French, and Spanish rivals did. Their smaller legacy is nevertheless very much a part of the Caribbean, and the natural salt of St. Martin, in a literal sense, helps to wash the shores of all the countries dubbed "Caribbean." Dr. Florian seems to be suggesting that the literature of this region, and the writings of Sekou in particular, can, and someday should, wash all of the region's literary shores.

There is an integrating intent in this book. She explores the influence that other Caribbean writers—including George Lamming, Kamau Brathwaite, Derek Walcott, Jamaica's dub poets, and others—have had on or reflects a kinship to the work of Lasana Sekou. She quotes from them to show the nature of their companionship in their literary endeavours. A well-known poet, fiction writer, journalist, social activist, educator, and nationalist for the independence of St. Martin, Sekou is no doubt already having, and will continue to have, an influence on writers from elsewhere in the region.

With its poverty, crime, and violence, the Caribbean is often "salt" in the Jamaican sense of the word. Dr. Florian challenges readers to agree or disagree with the extent to which it is also "salt" in Sekou's complex senses of the word. In my view, he seems to be one of those writers who believe that literature should help us to live our lives more abundantly, and to do so, he and his people, and the rest of us, need to find meaning in the salt mines of St. Martin, especially the Great Salt Pond, the largest and most significant of the island's salt-producing ponds during the time of Slavery, and which Sekou has called the "cradle of the nation" of St. Martin, "North" and "South."[1]

"Counterpoint" is defined as "music consisting of two or more melodic lines sounding simultaneously."[2] In a region famous for its music, a metaphor from this art form, combined with the metaphor of salt, promises to be a powerful combination. It suggests that there are a number of melodies running through the life and art of the Caribbean simultaneously. Dr. Florian describes the melodies she hears in Sekou's writings, and seeks to demonstrate how they harmonize with each other, as well as other literary and social melodies in the Caribbean. I am reminded of Rex Nettleford's view that Caribbean culture combines the rhythm of Africa and the melody of Europe. Dr. Florian may be concerned primarily with melodies, if she sticks to the definition, but it is evident that she is by no means tone-deaf to the rhythms, or *"riddims"* of the Caribbean, as she puts it, in keeping with the musical parlance of the region. J.S. Bach, a master of counterpoint in European music, is also famous for the dancing rhythms in his compositions.

Dr. Florian leaves us with the intriguing notion that there are simultaneous melodies of salt to be heard or imagined in the writings of Sekou. I think I detect snatches of the sorrowful melodies of Slavery-and-salt; and there are also rhythms of the life-giving property of the substance.

One of the fundamental philosophical questions that undergird the culture of the Caribbean is whether or not there is such a thing as a Caribbean aesthetic. As I understand it, those who ask this question are wondering if the arts of the Caribbean are surrounded by what Arthur Danto calls "an atmosphere of theory." This atmosphere would combine ideas about how the arts of the region should be described, analyzed, interpreted, and evaluated. It is a big question, and I have yet to see a comprehensive answer to it offered by anyone. Dr. Florian has an interest in the aesthetics of Caribbean poetry, and, in this book, she brings her research on this topic to bear on her examination of Sekou's work. This includes her examination of how Sekou's skills as a polyglot inform his work. She is interested in identifying the poetics that guide various elements of his work, including his versification and characterization. She is interested in how his aesthetic is related to his praxis as an activist and nationalist.

The aspect of Sekou's aesthetic that I find most interesting, as presented in this book, is his use of metaphor. Someone has said that a language is a collection of dead metaphors. If this is true, Sekou's metaphors, especially those of salt and music, could be in the process of contributing importantly to the growth of language in the Caribbean. His skills as polyglot, just mentioned, could be relevant here. One of my favorite definitions of poetry is that of a Native American people that says that poetry happens when words meet for the first time. In Sekou's writings, words from different languages may well be meeting for the first time, and who knows what kind of poetry may happen whenever this occurs?

I conclude with Hannah Arendt's view that metaphor is the device that poets use to reveal the oneness in the world. Suffering is part of our human oneness, whether it is caused by salt, sugar, "or whatever." Since we all need salt, it is therefore about not only the oneness of the Caribbean, but of all the world.

Earl McKenzie, PhD
Jamaica, 2019

Notes

[1] Lasana M. Sekou. *The Salt Reaper – poems form the flats.* St. Martin: House of Nehesi Publishers, 2005: 47-54.

[2] Willi Apel and Ralph Daniel. *The Harvard Brief Dictionary of Music.* New York: Washington Square Press, 1960.

INTRODUCING
THE POET AND HIS "I-LAND"

> *In the same language I live in*
> *I must rise up*
> *Among syllables of my parents*
> *In the land which I am*
> *And form*
> *A whole daughter a whole son*
> *Out of the Compromise*
> *Which I am*
>
> *To understand history*
> *I have to come home.*
>
> – E. McG. "Shake" Keane

Lasana Mwanza Sekou means poet, wise protector, warrior.[1] This name contains much of the essence of Sekou's writing in general but especially his poetry. He lived for thirteen years in the USA where he migrated to in the early 1970s from the island of St. Martin in the Caribbean. In New York he got to know the influential and revolutionary American author Amiri Baraka during his studies in political science/international relations at the State University of New York at Stony Brook. In Washington, DC, Sekou obtained his master's degree in mass communication from Howard University. In 1984, he returned home, to the Caribbean, to his "I-land" (a term from his poem "Nativity"), to his people.

The poet identifies with the St. Martin Land, which oozes so sweetly and painfully in his writings. He talks about the contemporaneity of the land and of the past, and of a liberated future. To the extent the present is often significantly a result of the past, in the case of the 37-square-mile island of St. Martin, the land issue is a major one. The island is divided into two parts, more or less by half, since the Treaty of Concordia in 1648, when French and Dutch colonizers divided the territory, too precious in commercial terms to be left to the other party. The "question of the land" is so important even nowadays that the issue of a territorial definition of "Saint-Martin/Sint Maarten" is still ongoing.[2] And since I love to dig in the etymology of words, and furthermore this might help us to understand who this place belongs to, we know that one of the first names reputedly given to this island was "Soualiga," Island Carib for "Land of Salt."[3]

The first settlers of the island can be placed sometime within the "Archeological reconstruction" mentioned in *Language, Culture, and Identity in St. Martin* (2014) by Dr. Rhoda Arrindell, which "suggests that the earliest evidence of human colonization in the Caribbean dates to around 3500 – 4000 BCE. All indications are that these people originated in Central America and are presumed to have been primarily hunters, gatherers, and fishing people." Many centuries after, when the time of the colonial explorations came and Europeans started to expand their trade routes, invasions, and wars of conquest around the world, the Dutch, skillful sailors, reached the coast of St. Martin in 1631, less than two decades before the Treaty of Concordia.

In his book *De Nederlanders in het Caraibische Zeegebied* (1942) *(The Dutch in the Caribbean Region)*, W.R. Menkman confirmed this year of the Dutch settlement, already famous for *"zeezout"* (sea salt); and in fact, the Dutch East India Company(VOC) traders loaded up salt at St. Martin to trade it back to Europe *("met de opdracht onderweg op Sint Maarten zout te laden")*,[4] where it was needed for sea voyages.

Menkman, thus, confirms the existence of a *"zoutvaart"* (marine salt trade) that made St. Martin a *"rijk"* ("rich") island, located in the northeast Caribbean and geographically in the Leeward Islands (but along with Saba and St. Eustatius they are also known as the "Dutch Windward Islands"), a sub-categorization of the Lesser Antilles. These terms "lesser" and "leeward" always imply a dichotomy ("greater" and "windward").

Starting over half a millennium ago, the Caribbean islands would come to be assembled like pawns on a chessboard of the colonial game. Menkman gives us a hint from the early records relative to the island: St. Martin was "rich" in something. Every island in the Caribbean had some sort of richness to exploit, from which to take profit. And St. Martin had salt, the Dutch West India Company knew it well. But even before the Dutch, there were French in the Northern part of the island, probably growing tobacco. If it was not for the Spanish memoirs and documents we probably would not have testimony of the land settlement, Menkman continues, because the Spanish came to St. Martin after the Dutch and the French and wanted a spotlight on the chessboard. Later on, the English invaded the island and took control.

It is obvious that the linguistic influences from these and other countries and peoples, including Africans, would have left a mark on the island's linguistic heritage: French, Dutch, Spanish, English and consequently in Sekou's poetry. Even Latin was used to conduct written negotiations with the "enemies" by the *"Senatus insulae S. Martini,"* "the Senate/government of the island of St. Maarten" in 1633, according to Menkman. Nowadays, following the tourism boom of the early 1970s that spurred much immigration to St. Martin, English, French, and Dutch are used alongside Haitian, Spanish, Papiamentu, and the other Creole/Kwéyòl languages of the Caribbean. Chinese, Sranan, Hindi, Arabic, Yoruba, Brazilian can be heard on the streets among other languages as well. But what is the political situation to date of St. Martin? As of 2007, the "Frenchside" or Northern part of St. Martin is a Collectivité d'outre-mer (COM) of France.⁵ The name of the territory carries the French spelling, and often enough the French pronunciation: "Saint-Martin." As of 2010, the Southern part or "Dutchside" of St. Martin is no longer an "island territory" of the (now dismantled) "Netherlands Antilles." It is instead a territory with an internal autonomy, with its parliament, within the Kingdom of the Netherlands.⁶ The name of the territory carries the Dutch spelling, but less often the Dutch pronunciation: "Sint Maarten."

The historical, language, and political realities of St. Martin are among the most fundamental reasons why Sekou's poetry is imbued with so many influences, spanning from Europe to North America to Africa and Asia. His poetic roots are "Glissantian," so wide as to resemble those of a mangrove. Nevertheless, his "Antillanity" or "Caribbeaness" is easily recognizable, as he encompasses other islands of the Caribbean archipelago and countries and territories of the region. Sekou's social interests are extended to all the world, although his most imminent concern is related to the political and cultural situation of St. Martin. "Love, Labor, Liberation" are the recurrent themes in Sekou's poetics (a detailed analysis on these has been done by the Montserratian literary scholar Howard Fergus). With these words Sekou sometimes signs his books, remarking on the leading themes of his life and work, so full of passion for women, of hard work, of political engagement for the liberation of his island, of solidarity with struggling humanity. These topics will be envisaged in this book, where I configure "an aesthetics of salt and sugar" as a (post)colonial and (post)plantation aesthetics,[7] able to embrace the whole literary production of the Caribbean.

Lasana M. Sekou is an original and fresh writer, and close to important contemporary writers of the region such as Shake Keane, David Rudder or AJA, and Kamau Brathwaite, to cite a few. As Fergus pointed out, "History is a motivator, but we must take responsibility for our future if we are to usher in new regimes of love."[8] Let's engage in this literary journey towards hope in a better future—be it in St. Martin or anywhere it is needed in the world—through a new and crisp understanding of the poetry and poetics of Sekou.

Sara Florian, PhD
Singapore, 2019

Notes

[1] The poet changed his name from Harold Hermano Lake to Lasana Mwanza Sekou in the mid-1970s, while attending the High School of Art and Design in New York City. Personal communication with the poet. E-mail. 6 July 2012. See also Askhari Hodari, Ph.D. *The African Book of Names*. Deerfield Beach, Florida: HCI: 2009: "Lasana or 'lah-SAH-nah' means poet (East Africa), 306. Mwanza or 'mwahzah' means wise protector (Central Africa), 220. Sekou means fighter or warrior (West Africa), 19."

² "The 37-square mile island is in actual fact divided between the Dutch and the French. The Dutch spelling 'Sint Maarten' was adopted in 1946, as a way of the colonialists claiming the 'Dutchness' of the part of the island that falls directly under Dutch rule. Before then, the whole island was referred to as 'Saint Martin' which is also the French spelling of the name purportedly given to the island by Christopher Columbus. (...) The official Dutch spelling however remains 'St. Maarten.'" Badejo, Fabian Adekunle. "Modern Literature in English in the Dutch Windward Islands: A Brief Introduction." *Calabash: A Journal of Caribbean Arts and Letters* 1.2 (Spring-Summer 2002): 77. I will hereafter adopt the spelling of St. Martin.

³ "Sualouiga, Oualichi (Sualouiga, also pronounced and written Souliaga or Soualiga, is thought to be an Island Carib word meaning 'Land of Salt.' Öualichi, also pronounced and written Qualichi, is said to be an Arawakan word meaning 'Land of Women' or 'Land of Brave Women.'" Sekou, Lasana M. *National Symbols of St. Martin*. 3.

⁴ *Cf.* Menkman, W.R. *De Nederlanders in het Caraibische Zeegebied waarin vervat de Geschiedenis der Nederlandsche Antillen*. 39.

⁵ *Cf.* Rutgers, Wim. "Dutch Caribbean Literature." 185-186.

⁶ *Cf.* MiVi associates. "Sint Maarten / Saint Martin - 10-10-10: New Country in the Dutch Kingdom."

⁷ Joseph H. Lake Jr. in his article, "Slavery and Independence" in *The Independence Papers, Volume 1* contrasted the idea that colonization is actually over by sustaining that "Plantation St. Maarten 1788" is equal to "Plantation St. Maarten 1988" and that the second will not become an independent country if not by the death of the former.

⁸ Fergus, Howard A. *Love Labor Liberation in Lasana Sekou*. 28.

AN AESTHETICS OF SALT AND SUGAR

> *Their cargoes of sponges*
> *On sandspits of islets,*
> *Barques white as white salt*
> *Of acrid St. Maarten.*
>
> – Derek Walcott, "A Sea-Chantey"

Literature is not merely concerned with writing. It is even less concerned with writing for its own sake. The encounter with Lasana M. Sekou's work forms a literary engagement, and as such, "Lasana does not practice *l'art pour l'art*"[1]: it is instead significantly invested in tangible needs. Perhaps because of this, particularly once we are introduced to his poetry and fictions, we may find it difficult, at times even uncomfortably so, to avoid reading him, listening to him, to avert our eyes from gazing at his performances. The eminent Caribbean thinker and author George Lamming observed:

> Sekou believes that your literature is not about literature. Literature is about people in movement and people in the transformation of society and so on.[2]

The evocation of the elements of history, culture, and landscapes to tell the stories of the people of St. Martin; the complex of humanity that is portrayed provides the power that makes his work compelling.

Sekou is a poet, short story writer, essayist, author of dramatic monologues and historical profiles, and journalist from the Caribbean island of St. Martin.[3] Derek Walcott, recognizing the origin of his Dutch maternal grandfather from the Dutch part or southern half of St. Martin,[4] in "A Sea-Chantey" notes that the island was known as a source of salt.[5] Sekou himself was called "el 'Walcott' del Caribe holandés,"[6] "the Walcott of the Dutch Caribbean" by essayist and theologian Dr. Armando Lampe. Sekou's verse is not classical in the way that Walcott's is, but his love for the word gives his witty poems, subtle riddles, and encyclopedic references as broad a spectrum as the bard of St. Lucia. Further, in Sekou, who is likely closer in the poetic aspect and *riddim* to Kamau Brathwaite than he is to Walcott, a recurring theme underlies all of his productions: salt.

Brathwaite spoke of a "submarine unity" among the islands, referring to a cultural set of musical and historical rhythms that accompanied those ancestors who were forced to cross the Middle Passage and reach the Caribbean bound in chains on board slave ships. This musicality is found today in all Caribbean poetry, whether within circular, strong rhythms in Brathwaite's poetry, in the beauty and mystery of the St. Lucian landscape in Walcott, or bubbling out of the mud of St. Martin's Great Salt Pond and other marshes in Sekou. It is as if those rhythms/*riddims*, traveling with the enslaved people, crossed the ocean underwater and continued to re-emerge out of the waters of the islands, through cultural expressions, such as writing, music, song, art, carnival or theater, and dance. These rhythms are like echoes of a long-gone memory as it comes home to its people.

Salt is to Sekou what the image of Namsetoura is to Brathwaite. They are both what, in 1844 on the French island colony of Réunion—previously called Bourbon—Louis Timagène Houat called *"le génie de l'endroit."*[7] They are sacred spirits of the place and connect to poets to save their historical memory from being lost and forgotten. They ask with "salty" words to be defended and remembered. Thus, the poets sing about their homes because they feel both a poetic responsibility as well as a social one to those places, memories, and ancestors. Memory must be continually revived and kept alive so that the historical trauma is not forgotten and a better future is evolved.

On salt and sugar

Salt was the main product of St. Martin at the peak of salt-picking on the island, between 1792 and 1797 and between 1817 and 1961[8]; it is present both in the south and the north of the 37-square-mile island; and it is an important part of the natural ecosystem.[9]

The origin of the modern English word "salary" comes from the Latin *sāl / salis*,[10] which is cognate with the Greek ἅλς / ἁλός (*háls / halós*).[11] Salt was a precious product and a vital part of trade, from China to Rome to the Kingdom of Mutapa. At one time, Roman soldiers were paid in salt, thus the origin of the modern English word salt. One of the most important Roman roads in Italy was called the via Salaria, the Salt Road. The development of the entire region of Northern Italy and modern Austria, beginning around the fifth to fourth centuries BCE, revolved around the salt trade, as did the rise of the maritime republics of Genoa and Venice and the growth of the Salzkammergut region, where Salzburg is located. The salt trade was vital for the entire Mediterranean Basin,[12] and the trade of salt stretched from Northern Europe to the Trans-Saharan routes and even to East Asia.

Salt has deep roots in world history, in trade and in the sea. In Sekou's poetry, these connections are enhanced and reach out to the land itself and God, in various forms, from ancient times onwards. In the St. Martin migration poem "boats" in *Mothernation – Poems from 1984 to 1987* (1991), Sekou recalls the slave crops: "and ven boats didn't tek back tobacco / dey tek cotton and sugar / dey tek salt / den dey tek us, salt of the earth, again." The expression "salt of the earth" is also used by Jesus in the Gospel of Matthew (5:13):

> You are the salt of the earth. But if the salt loses its saltiness, how can it be made salty again? It is no longer good for anything, except to be thrown out and trampled underfoot.[13]

These lines not only indicate Christian doctrine but also show the importance of salt and its deep ties with relationships and spiritual beliefs. Sekou's poetry expresses spirituality and the experiences of Atlantic Slavery, and it is also entrenched in the land and the liberation of the lands and peoples of the New World from post-Columbian invaders and colonizers.

The expression salt of the earth may be a metaphor that relates to the preciousness of the people who are laboring the land, but it also relates to the Slavery that tore people from one land and unloaded them on another. Of course, salt also plays a role in feeding. In Sekou's poetry, salt enhances the body and the soul, which is the self and the "i&i," and heals with its power. This power to nurse an oppressed nature back to life and to the awareness of the self, Brathwaite's X/Self, is given place as an essential element or force in the folklore and supernatural world of the Caribbean region. In *Voodoo* (1959) by Alfred Métraux and *Crónicas Caribeñas* (2012) by Alejo Carpentier, we are reminded that for those who exploit zombies, salt is a dangerous food. The smallest grain or barest taste of salt would awaken in the zombies an awareness of their human minds. Then, the oppressed creatures would turn against their masters—with fatal consequences for them.

Salts are formed when a base and an acid react to, and neutralize, each other to create an ionic compound; to transpose this scientific truth into a very imaginative metaphor, we could interpret St. Martin as the base in this compound and the atrocity and the sour aftermath of Slavery as the acid part. The salt ponds in this image are a reaction to this historical combination. Sea salt passes through a curious process; salt dissolves in water, but then, the sea water becomes saturated with it and produces it through an osmotic process in a salty concentration. The salt of memory thus pervasively oozes out of the historical memory of a place, culturally, spiritually, and chemically, and Sekou identifies this natural symbol as a symbol of Slavery. Salt is used to preserve food, to give sapidity, and to heal/purify. Sekou's verse preserves the memory of St. Martin (its *quimbé* song or *ponum* dance), gives meaning to the laments of the spirits of the place, and tries, in this poetic and aesthetic way, to purify the pain of this heritage to build a new country.

Sekou engages in this quest—the search for a geographically and historically healed and unified island nation—in his linguistic choices by using a salty and salted language, which is soaked in creole and different languages, all mixed together on the island of St. Martin and encountered in his travels. Walcott, using maritime metaphors relating to his native St. Lucia, also soaked his language in sea salt and referred to the language of the people of St. Lucia. As Walcott admitted in the poem "The Schooner Flight" from his 1979 work *The Star-Apple Kingdom*, "when I write / this poem, each phrase go be soaked in salt / I go draw and knot every line as tight / as roped in this rigging; in simple speech / my common language go be the wind." Walcott insisted more than once in his career on the need for a simple, new, fresh, Adamic language to create a new island epic. In "Gros-Islet," published in *The Arkansas Testament* (1987), he describes how "From this village, soaked like a grey rag in salt-water, / a language came, garnished with conch shells." To the conch shells, Sekou adds the abengs, the shells/horns used by Caribbean and South American maroons to communicate with one another.

The voice of the poet of St. Martin is not only soaked in the island's waters but also in his travels around the world. He engages in a political fight for St. Martin, adding his voice to the struggle for freedom and justice for those without a voice in African and American countries and on other Caribbean islands. In the strophe "Culture is all over," in his *Nativity* (1988, 2010), Sekou seeks to rally the power of the people to

> STAND FIRM
> &
> FORWARD ON

in his solidarity with "The People,"

> who reclaiming ground & victorying on
> who never screw up face & skin up teeth
> at ground & scorn the liberating rites of passage

This commitment reminds us of that of the Tobagonian poet Eric Roach, when, in "Senghor Visiting," he addresses the visiting Senegalese poet Léopold Sédar Senghor with these lines: "languages jostle in the mosaic […] / come back to salt the tongue."

The idea of a creative relationship between language and salt is expressed in the very title of the book *Salted Tongues—Modern Literature in St. Martin* by Fabian Adekunle Badejo. The "crop of new literary voices" identified by Badejo in St. Martin in this 2003 collection of essays is likened to "the harvest of salt from this pond thought to have become barren." As an item needed to heal wounds, Meredith Gadsby observed in *Sucking Salt: Caribbean Women Writers, Migration, and Survival* (2006) that "sucking salt carries a simultaneously doubled linguistic sign of adversity and survival," a survival of centuries of Slavery and suffering. As the Montserratian historian and poet Howard Fergus put it, "salt hurts and heals."[14]

In Sekou, salt is an expression of what is needed to survive, to heal the wounds created by history, and to speak. This is the landmark in Sekou's aesthetics that helps one to orient around the rest. In this use of salt as a metaphor for the past and the present and to project oneself toward the future, Sekou makes contact with the deeper meaning of words and texts made of words in what Julia Kristeva calls the "thetic phase." No post-structuralist or any other theories are applied here to Sekou, but I find Kristeva's analogy fitting. When she speaks about the meaningfulness of the text, she also claims that a text is an "echo" of the past and a "forerunner" of the future; it is a "collision between 'before' and 'after.'"[15] She associates with this "thetic phase" two other events that contribute to define it: the mirror stage and the discovery of castration.

When Sekou confronts the Great Salt Pond in St. Martin as a poet and describes it as a mirror of the island's history, he at the same time separates the salt pond as an object from its meaning. He creates a reflection of a past event that takes the form of a detached imaginary, and he conglobates the past and the present of the island, creating an image that is pointed toward the future of the nation. This second event does not concern Sekou himself as he does not detach from his mother(land)'s body; instead, even if he describes the island as a place of pleasure, he sticks to the cause and returns to the island after his travels. Sekou's thetic phase thus lies between the pre-colonial semiotic drive and the postcolonial symbolic articulation; his tongue, like a stake, seeks and describes a new, brash reality in an extemporaneous and durable poetry.

Sekou's travel between salt as a dominant aesthetics in his work, and sugar, which is dominant in the aesthetics and economics in all language zones of Caribbean literature and studies of plantation history, is also indicative of how, with his foundational trinity of themes that are the focus of Fergus's *Love Labor Liberation in Lasana Sekou* (2007), he sticks to the underpinning and returns to the native element of salt.

Cuban scholar and author Emilio Jorge Rodríguez notes that at the basis of the plantation economic system in the Caribbean region was the norm of the sugar plantations but that the island of St. Martin was an exception to this. St. Martin's historical reality is thus itself responsible for the omnipresence of salt in Sekou's poetry and its importance to his poetics, particularly when it is reckoned that salt was not a main product in the rest of the Caribbean, with its place being taken by sugar. Of course, sugar was cultivated in St. Martin, and as Rodríguez observed, it was not until 1630 that the colonizers began to focus on the island's salt ponds.[16] At the time, the Slavery-dependent sugar industry in the region was already nearing the end of its first 100 years of sweet "bread for merciless slavers" and for the brutally enslaved, "bitter lice bite crumbs for you."[17]

The word sugar comes from the Latin *saccharum / saccharii*[18] and Greek σάκχαρ, σάκχαρος (*sákkhar / sákkharos*)[19] by way of Arabic *assokkar / shuker* and eventually from the Sanskrit *çàrkarâ*, which means grains of sand. Thus, both salt and sugar bear a relation to the sea and sand. In the Caribbean, after the introduction of sugar plantations by the Spanish and the Portuguese, it would become the main crop in Saint-Domingue, Cuba, Jamaica, Barbados, and Guyana. In the Antilles, the production of sugar took off due in no small part to Dutch dominance in the slave trade: they were major traders both in Asia, through the Dutch East India Company, and in the Americas, through the Dutch West India Company. The main crops traded were tobacco, salt, and sugar.[20]

In his *Coming, Coming Home—Conversations II*, Lamming reminds us that Europe, "by the eighteenth century, had transformed sugar into the value of steel and oil in our time."[21] In Sekou's work, even before *Mothernation*, the theme of salt and the sugar industry found their place relative to Slavery and the plantation system in the five dramatic monologues that followed the long poem "Nativity" in *Nativity and monologues for today* (1988). These monologues tackled memories of olden times and the modern problems of St. Martin society. The characters recounting their memories of these events in these narratives are Great Grandmother T, a hotel maid, a casino man, a student, and a woman. The casino man, or casino dealer, is the one who discusses sugar and salt, in reference to Slavery and the plantation system:

> Big house or wattle dung hut, it is still slavery, and all ah we still on this plantation. And after sugar industry gone sour and the cotton blow 'way; and the salt dry up; and pott rum close down.

In my first interview with him, Sekou noted that in his poems he metabolized the symbols of salt and sugar, relating them to different modes of expression. He drew in part on historical data, his own experiences, and other elements and features to develop a diverse range of spiritual and cultural meanings for these symbols—including the use of a Yoruba idiom told to him by Badejo:

> It should be natural for the salt metaphor to be present in the literature of St. Martin. Salt was the main crop on the island during the unholy slave period.... As metaphor and as material salt has the experience of curing, preserving, healing. There is a connection to life's sweetness in some cultures. The

Yoruba, I am told, have a saying: "May your life be as sweet as salt." It is also intrinsically connected with the exploitation and human suffering of the enslaved ancestors that toiled away in the salt ponds of St. Martin.... *The Salt Reaper* poems "salt reaping I" and "salt reaping II" are about this double and layered relationship of salt in the history and culture of the St. Martin people and as a recurring expression of the psyche, even if latently so, at the core of the nation. Both poems are sorts of aesthetic extractions from a conversation, a relate, with a rather beautiful woman from Sucker Garden *[district of St. Martin]* who worked in the Great Salt Pond as a very young child during the first half of the last century.[22]

With reference to Sekou's work, sugar and the sweetness of salt collide in his poetry, and this collision is part of the poignancy of his poetry, itself forming the quest of liberation for his *mothernation*. Before Sekou, in the written poetry of St. Martin, its history of salt, the salt pond, and sea salt were for all intents and purposes negligible to nonexistent. Now the salt metaphor is increasingly used, particularly when it is linked to the ponds of St. Martin, in both poetry and art. This is arguably the result of the intensity and complexity of Sekou's sustained oral and written narratives—the sort of foundation that he laid down, mostly between *Born Here* (1986), his first poetry collection published in St. Martin, and the landmark book *National Symbols of St. Martin—A Primer* (1996, 1997) that he edited and his widely read 1996 poem "Great Salt Pond Speaks." Sekou's output exploits the *intentio operis* (Umberto Eco's concept of the voluntary and the involuntary meaning of a text) to signify his understanding of culture and tradition. Thus, from the way in which other St. Martin poets and artists have taken to juxtaposing salt, saltwater, and the sweet, even if they do not directly mention sugar, they clearly identify it this way, centering their island's salt and salt history in their work.

In Esther Gumbs's debut poetry collection, *Tales From the Great Salt Pond* (1996), the opening poem "First Ancient People," speaks of "soualiaga / exercising her magnificent water-beds of salt." However, in the lamentation "Salt Pond," the poet hears the distress of that body of water and remembers:

> once sun shone upon you
> once full moon made love over you
> banklakes purified by salt
> but you were sweet.

The cover of Gumbs's work by David Kobelt, a striking painting of a Namsetoura, a spirit emanating from the mangroves—a blazing sun at its back—and licking the pond waters haunts the reader.

The pond and the sea, being "baptized by salt water," "a grain of sand," and "amniotic" fluids are among the references to salt, sustained throughout the books *The Rainy Season* (1997) and *skin* (2006) by Drisana Deborah Jack. Badejo considers Jack to be a revolutionary poet. Charles Borromeo Hodge, whose verse approaches a classical meter, writes of "silver mirror ponds" in his sole collection *Songs & Images of St. Martin* (1997).

In 1999, the St. Martin musician Neville York released *Sweet Salt—contemporary & classical steel pan music*, his first audio CD. Marta Dijkhoff, the minister of culture and education of the later-dissolved Netherlands Antilles, called the album "clear and articulate as salt crystals."[23] According to the writer Camille Baly, with *Sweet Salt*, "Neville has extended the coming together around the salt pond into a congregation in the Pan Basin."[24]

Modern interpretations in dance and storytelling are also juxtaposing the island's salt and salt history with cultural works created in twenty-first century. In "The salt metaphor in St. Martin's literature," my interview with Sekou published at House of Nehesi Publishers website (2009), the poet pointed out that:

"The dancer and choreographer Clara Reyes has been making dramatically bold and informed performance pieces relative to this business of salt in our history and culture." In the article, "Tribute to great salt pond, activism, heritage, and tears" (Pearlfmradio.sx, 2011), we read that St. Martin's "Nicole de Weever, the Broadway star of *Fela!* fame, choreographed and danced to the recital of 'Cradle of the Nation'…. She received a strong dance accompaniment by Rudy Davis." As for the old art form of storytelling, the "Salt pond Goddess" is a new tale that takes place in the Great Salt Pond, written and performed regularly by "Papa Umpo" (Garfield Young), a St. Martin teacher and storyteller.[25]

The Frock & Other Poems (2010), a posthumous publication by folklorist Laurelle "Yaya" Richards, features "Abandoned Salt Pond," a spellbinding account of the last generation to pick salt in the "sweet salt pond" of Grand Case, at the end of what Sekou terms St. Martin's Traditional Period (1848–1963). From among the works of 25 poets in *Where I See the Sun—Contemporary Poetry in St. Martin* (2013), edited by Sekou, at least six reference salt in their poems in reference to St. Martin, or to the island's Amerindian name "soualiga," to culture, history, identity, ponds, the sea, and other aspects of the land and its people. This anthology includes both newer and more senior writers, including some of those who contributed to the St. Martin salt issue in the collection: Tamara Groeneveldt, Tadzio Bervoets, Jay B. Haviser, Jack, and Faizah Tabasamu (Rochelle Ward), who, in "soualiga," claims that:

> i know her
> i come from her belly
> lived on her body
> smelt the yeasting of her pond

and Raymond Helligar, whose often-recited and well-received "'Sin' Martin Is We'z Own," sings of:

> ... this sweet sugar and sea cotton island [...]
>
> We who planted the fields of enslavers, [...]
> We grew their crops, we reaped their salt
> We labor from dusk to dawn in those salt ponds

Contemporary Caribbean poets, including AJA from Barbados, Kendel Hippolyte from St. Lucia, and Andrea Hutchinson from Jamaica, also have their own unique bittersweet elements in their verse and demand justice and liberation from cultural, political, and economic oppression in their writings. These bittersweet voices carry similar overtones; however, Sekou attempts a broader appeal, aspiring to the liberation of the Brathwaitian X/Self to what

Martinique's Édouard Glissant calls "wordliness," or what noted economist Norman Girvan would call globalization and openness to a common consideration of the Caribbean.

This interpenetration of salt and sugar or the exploration of the sweetness of salt can be seen in Fergus's observation that "salt is St. Martin's sugar."[26] These collisions and interpenetrations are not limited to this emblematic duality of the sweet and salty as found in the island's history and that of its people but have a weightier symbolic freight. In an early poem by Sekou, "My Boy Told Me," sugar and salt bear erotic overtones and lead to a sensual double-meaning in *For The Mighty Gods... An Offering* (1982): "If you will need my sugar / While on your journey [...] / Besides you have a salt pill to equalize / The excess sugar water." This is not the only time that Sekou writes of salt or salt and sugar in a romantic overture—another example is the line "on a salted beach" in "Womanage" from his *Born Here*. However, it is when Sekou mixes salt and sugar with St. Martin and Caribbean pre- and post-Emancipation history and culture and modern wordliness or societal issues that he is the most adept at linking the symbology of sugar to his overriding theme of salt and likening the St. Martin idea of sweet to his own aesthetics of salt.

The salt pyramids of St. Martin

In the times of Slavery, salt reaping was performed by hand. To quote Sekou again from my interviews with him:

> The enslaved salt-reapers collected the salt crystals from the waters of the Great Salt Pond, Grand Case Pond, and the other comparatively smaller salt lakes of St. Martin. The salt was then transported on wooden, tray-like flat boats, the "flats," to the shores or banks of the ponds. There, the bondsmen, women, and children reloaded the salt by hand in buckets, straw baskets or smaller trays, hoisted those on their heads or on the heads of each other, walked to and eventually onto ladder-like steps aside the mound of salt as it increased to pile on or pile up the salt in "heaps." In St. Martin, these heaps were never far from the beach or seashore—where the grueling process of reloading and unloading to the boats anchored in, for example, Great Bay Harbor, would start all over again.[27]

Two of Sekou's collections particularly pertinent to the element of salt and its processual and symbolic impact on the human body and psyche in his idea of the core of the nation, are: *The Salt Reaper—poems from the flats* (2004, 2005) and *37 Poems* (2005). A verse in *37 Poems* speaks of the configuration of the island in relation to salt and sugar, namely, "st. martin soul II": "when it raise up in you / sweetly so and salty too / [...] from hills through flats / [...] races you down hills, dunk you in pond stink & sweet." This had already been further developed, in the poetic persona of the figure of the pond itself, which speaks to the task of salt reaping, in "Great Salt Pond Speaks," from *The Salt Reaper*: "I come from creation. Teeming with life. Sifted salt from hillside majesty; kept beach a virgin garden [...] I am the mudbag reservoir of your labor / [...] floating over my glass calm face on flats."

In this poem, the Great Salt Pond recalls salt-reapers sifting salt, but a contraposition between the swarming of life and labor occurs here, between active movement and the flatness of the calm surface of the pond. Sekou's poems often take on the social plague of prostitution, and even here, the beach or the shore, which serves as a platform for the storage of salt, sounds like a "bitch"; notwithstanding this, it looks like a "virgin garden." The "Great Salt Pond Speaks" rests on a pathetic fallacy, recognizing the presence of a historical voice, a type of soul, inhabiting the pond, a Namsetoura. In both of these poems, the salt pond, with its long history of suffering, is depicted in its contemporary role of a dump, where "rubbage" (a neologism for rubbish or garbage used by Sekou) is thrown: as the pond gurgles, "From reservoir of salt […] / I am the stink of town: the nation's stench and scorn. / Septic trucks haul up like chamber pot."

Sekou uses salt as a symbol to speak of the past of Slavery, which he not only relates to the reality of St. Martin but also extends to many countries around the world, largely African ones.

The "Great Salt Pond Speaks" is a case in point for the poet's extension of references beyond St. Martin. This poem was published in *The Salt Reaper* but was written 8 years previously. The winning Carnival queen of 1996, Shirley Serbony, was the first to dramatically recite the poem as her talent segment before a Carnival Village audience.[28]

The poet recited it himself a number of times between 1996 and 2017, on and off the island, from the Caribbean to China. The poem discusses the flats, ferrying salt across the pond waters to the shore, and the heaps of salt that created pyramidical shapes on the pond banks: "salt-cauterized feet, rapine of skin / […] reaping pyramids of salt for the red, white, and blue […] / From salt crystals of purple glow in harvest." Salt cauterizes the wounds of people pressed into servitude, when the entire process of Slavery is echoed in those three words "rapine of skin." A plethora of colors invades these few lines, with the tar of the skins of the enslaved people piling up pyramids of white salt, mounting up in three colors and shadowed in the purple glow of the crystals in the water. The red, white, and blue are the colors of the flags of the Netherlands and of France, the two nations that split St. Martin between them in 1648. The meaning of the colors and the colors themselves are now lost in the rubbish that is filling up the pond. Rubbish is something that we throw away.

In "cradle of the nation," a poem from *The Salt Reaper* that the Jamaican cultural critic Dr. Carolyn Cooper has called "magisterial,"[29] Sekou screams together with the pond—using a line grafted in from "Great Salt Pond Speaks"—to preserve this historical memory and not to allow it to pass on with a disdainful "Cheeeeeeeeeeeeee! Nasty Salt Pond. Go / away!"

In *National Symbols of St. Martin*, Sekou reminded the reader in prose that the pyramids mentioned in *The Salt Reaper* are "patterned after the shape of harvested salt ('salt heaps') when salt-picking was consistently the island's single largest industry before and after 1848."[30] This image of a pyramid may invoke the pyramids in Giza in St. Martiners and in many of us around the world and bring to life their construction by the labor of an enslaved and captive people. However, the poet does not let the reader remain long with this Biblical symbolism, which is linked to an ancient African kingdom along the Nile. He returns the symbol to the banks of the Great Salt Pond, to the reality of "reaping pyramids of salt for the red, white, and blue/slave kingdoms"[31] the salt that cauterized the wounds of enslaved men, women, and children was also the salt that created them in the first place, as noted in the short poem "1" from *Quimbé – Poetics of Sound* (1991):

> It was pain
> in this labor among saline blades
> cutting into our blood
> to reap pyramids of salt.

Sekou, thus, employs tangible and sometimes harsh metaphors to shake the reader and awaken the conscience to the harsh reality of the past. Nonetheless, in his concrete lines, he conjures the spirits of place and is constantly in search of his own way to awareness and that of the reader to closely approach an improved spiritual self, the "i&i." The enslaved people figured in the pond resemble the Douens of the Trinidadian poet and artist LeRoy Clarke, who brought into his poems these afflicted characters of a derelict society.[32] This pond of St. Martin is a sort of *douendom*,[33] a derelict mini-kingdom where empty slaves and puppets blend with water in a profane baptism and are emptied of their bodily fluids. Interestingly, Clarke employed the pyramid image in his painting *Eye image I* and to describe the enhancement of the awareness of the self by climbing the ladder of the douendom and opening up to knowledge of the inner self, the eye/I.[34]

In Sekou, the pyramid of salt, constructed with Slavery and suffering, becomes a geometrical output, indicating the deep connection between the experience of Slavery linking through a double path of ascent to the tip. On the one side, Sekou's poetry bridges the past and the present, continually localized in his commitment even while he is open to the world for his engagement to its reality.

On the other hand, the experience of Slavery is intermingled with the reality of *marronage*, describing how enslaved people escaped from their plantations for short periods, long ones, and forever; likewise, how they continually attacked the plantocracy through nocturnal raids on the *habitation* or *établissement*,[35] the house and associated fields or setting them on fire. The reality of *marronage* will be examined in the following chapter, but here it should be noted that in Sekou's poetry, one idea strongly emerges strong: cultural *marronage* still exists, and it constitutes one avenue leading to and revolutionizing political independence.

Sekou is never far from the political in any of his writings, nor does he ever sacrifice the aesthetics of culture to it. The American critic Dr. Ervin Beck may have been thinking of this feature while writing his review of *The Salt Reaper* in *World Literature Today* (March–April 2006: 58-59):

> His calibanic voice moves between the public, revolutionary political rhetoric of Linton Kwesi Johnson and the lush, esoteric wordplay of Dylan Thomas.

As noted above, Sekou's poetry is full of spirituality. It is as if through the aspiration for independence, the self, as citizen and poet, and as the descendant of the enslaved among others, acquires a spiritual knowledge. This is a liberating experience of love.

There is a recognizable spirituality to the Great Salt Pond that results in its poetic persona. This aspect is developed by lines from "cradle of the nation" that describe the waters of the pond as a baptismal font. In this poem from *The Salt Reaper*, the sacred blends with the profane blend, in the way that Christianity was imposed by the colonizers onto those they enslaved, who "would be baptized in the pit of/salt/ spit piss semen&sweat. [...] / a lake of brine, mirror the splinter of this crime of centuries [...] / past the saltpicking [...] / borne on the fresh and sweet stink."

In "Great Salt Pond Speaks" the pond suddenly becomes a mirror in which the slaves sweat due to their brutal labor, and at the same time it becomes a shroud:

> Through briny ages, I was the pot of water
> in which you first saw your sweat-drenched face,
> anchored your sweating ebon brow under a crown
> of thorns.
> In the blowing season, the salt I bore was stock [...]
> It was you who sowed humanity in me with the
> bleeding

Leaving aside the ethnicity or ethnic background of Jesus Christ in this image, one could critique that the imposition of Christianity onto generations of people who were forced to abandon their gods and their spiritualities, although in a cruel irony they exhibited the life of Christ. Consequently, the reference here to a crown of thorns recalls Christ, and this allusion re-emerges with the cross of salt in "the sin," a poem from *37 Poems*: "prickling deep&seep on a cross of salt? / time to heal yourself."

Salt, as a healer, is also a seasoning too. Sekou is not alone in acknowledging this among this perspective, among a commanding host of Caribbean literary and artistic voices identified in *The Salt Reaper*, among those who:

> keep/a/count/in hurricane voices / in a shanty sing in a Quimbé ring / dem inna wukkershout riddim: / *How dey say salt pond dead,* / [...]salt-picking hands, choked red shreds of fingers / (but I had seasoned you, my son)[36]

In *Salt: A Novel* (1996), Earl Lovelace uses salt "to season our minds" as Hollis "Chalkdust" Liverpool mentions in his introduction to *The Salt Reaper*. Liverpool, a Trinidad and Tobago kaisonian and professor, calls Sekou the "salt reaper" who "in 2004, gives us *The Salt Reaper* to provide salt for all of us." Liverpool's introduction is powerful, and it foregrounds salt as a seasoning for Caribbean intellectuals. Fergus, instead, brings out a metaphor related to another of Lovelace's books, *The Wine of Astonishment*, observing how "Sekou... has matured beyond his years.... He was turning water and St. Martin's salt into the wine of literary astonishment."[37] *The Salt Reaper* is a book of salt, made of salt, seasoned, cooked, served, and foregrounding the importance of salt in the history of St. Martin.

Salt that seasons the memory also appears as a major theme and central to the material in the art of Jack. In "Unearthing Memories: A Conversation with St. Martin Artist Deborah Jack," the artist and poet calls salt "a strategic metaphor":

> St. Martin has this "Great Salt Pond" where slaves were brought to work. This pond has since become a landfill for garbage... This idea of the dirtying/the sullying of the pond can be linked to the suppression/oppression of memory.... That is why I use salt as a strategic metaphor.... There were moments when the pond would stink... In the summer of 2002 I had an exhibit at the Bearden Gallery in St. Martin where I actually applied salt to the canvas, and then painted in grids, these works were called the "A/Salting Series," and these grid-like structures have a direct connection to the salt pond that was also gridded, aerial photographs show that the pond is divided up into squares and rectangles.... St. Martin was called "souligia" *[ed. Soualiga]* at one point, which was the old Carib name for the island, and this meant island of salt. So salt was really strong for even the indigenous people.[38]

The writers and artists who take into account or bring out in their work salt in its seasoning aspect in relationship to the healing power of an aesthetics of salt are not exhausted here of course. Gadsby, for example, reviews writings related to salt produced by other Caribbean writers: *The Salt Roads* by Nalo Hopkinson, *Feeding the Ghosts* by Fred D'Aguiar, and *Black Salt* by Glissant. The peoples of the Caribbean Sea region adopt the intake and expression of this seasoning in their cultural and literary arts, which ultimately may very well be essential to metabolizing the substance of Brathwaite's idea of a submarine unity and Walcott's *History is Sea*.

The surfaces that Brathwaite and Walcott refer to, the lower and upper ones, respectively, of the same seas, are as much in flux in Sekou's aesthetics of salt as the canyons of brine that he describes at the bottom of the Great Salt Pond and the face of its waters, which can turn to "still sheets of glass," as described in *The Salt Reaper*. For Sekou, the sea and the waters of the Great Salt Pond are indispensable for a St. Martin or Caribbean aesthetic of salt, and they are acknowledged for this in his poetry, drama, and fiction. The starkest similarity appears where the sea, like the pond, appears as a baptismal font in Sekou's fiction. This occurs in "A Salting," the opening novella of *Brotherhood of the Spurs* (1997, 2007). After an arduous journey, the child that Nana Mandisa is traveling with, a cherished African child, her father's "wide-eyed-tickle-of-a-daughter," reaches the West Indies, and after having her first menses, in a sense, she is baptized in and by the Caribbean waters. In this story, bodily fluids mingle with the waters of the ocean during the Middle Passage crossing aboard the slave vessel *Snelheid Willem*.

In Sekou, the waters of St. Martin are a reservoir of sweat, tears, mucus, vomit, milk, urine, blood, and water. Salt is within and upon the water, held in the air, and found everywhere. The story "A Salting" treats these issues in a more complex way, however, depicting chained Africans as already looking for freedom as they approach and first see the island that will hold them. Some plan to run, like maroons, into the hills. Bound in the unlit hull of the slave ship is a warrior belonging the child's people. He is one of three sentinels that her father, a chief judge, had sent to guard her and the traveling party of the elderly midwife and seer, Nana Mandisa. They had been sailing downriver to the western coast of "God's Land," where Nana had been summoned to midwife a "promised birth." Their craft was attacked by slave raiders, and after a fierce fight, the sentinel was also captured, and his fellow sentinels were fatally shot. Still the warrior, he calls out to the distressed, menstruating girl:

> Little sister in my charge... This morning ... when they pitched us with salt water from the Great Sea and whipped us to dance...we saw hills of this S'maatin Lan'. The blessing of green peaks were sweet unto our eyes. [...] When you know this land, run far into it. No land or time is without hiding places.

The protagonist of the story has left her native land, a not too large West African trading city (where incidentally salt is a major trans-Saharan trade product), for the first time. This journey coincides with her passage to womanhood, and it marks a large change in the girl's life. Her passage to Slavery is underlined by a passage to a new way of living, with other captives from other peoples, tribes, and nations, with different languages, being forced to adopt a new religion, in a new land where her eventual baptism in the salt pond will reveal her new way of life. As the ship crosses the Atlantic Ocean toward St. Martin, through the Caribbean Sea, even while the enslaved, the slavers, and the sailors on board smell the wind-borne salt, and the vessel heads about Great Bay Harbor, Sekou situates the child in "A Salting" as an iconic persona, to be baptized in the Great Salt Pond, a progenitor of St. Martiners.[39]

In "cradle of the nation" from *The Salt Reaper*, the baptizing water is fertilized with bodily fluids, but unlike in the depths of the sea, the added constant of returning and repeating movements in the waters of the pond appears. The concentration and graphically described movements are gripping. In his other poems as well, descriptions of the activities of the enslaved pass through a magnifying glass, which makes the scorching weather hideous on the back of the salt pickers and expands their body parts: wounded hands, sweaty bent backs, and cracked heels are spotlighted in the depiction of the surface of the pond. In "saline," published in *Quimbé* this is given as "picking hands / greased by tears of sweat / and ooze of blood / […] to lift our feet / in and out the saltpans of great bay and grand case." From "st. martin children I," in *37 Poems*, "the sea / washes your feet bare to deep-steep. the salt."

The poet takes the images from salted waters to the village of "middle region," also in *37 Poems*: "what splash won't thirst for salt feet will drink the rest / […] you got to pound salt crack open locust to eat from yellow powder sprinkling fo' food to grow up." Then to expose "the divided of the nation" with his "claim" in *The Salt Reaper:* "its making fresh, salt heap and bled rip skin / in bitter soak, in the great basin of purple brine." The movements of the salt pickers in the pans are circular and undulating, like those of the waves on the sea. In the lines above, all from short poems, almost as short as Japanese haikus, Sekou describes the movements of salt pickers from the past and current periods of the island's reality. The poems "salt reaping I" and "salt reaping II" from *The Salt Reaper* recount and reflect respectively on the experiences of a woman from Sucker Garden, who worked in the salt pans of Great Bay (traditional name for Philipsburg) in the early part of the twentieth century:

> going down&going in
> was sweet
> but the work, o
> was hell.

This event, which occurred 100 years after Emancipation, when pastoral St. Martiners were paid little for picking salt for export, appears here in a piece that resembles a song. It also appears that the poet aims, in his reflection, to transform the harshness of this experience into an experience of love:

> we keep hearing now
> it was sweet but hard
> maybe so
> it was like loving.

As in a song, and echoing both the experience of the salt picker and contemplation of the poet, the voices of the enslaved forebears of both are evoked in the verses.

The *voice* is that of the sea, the pond, the lagoon (mentioned in "A Salting" as a place where slaves could be smuggled into St. Martin). The voice is that of a vessel as it is bearing on the water the blood and tears of human suffering and dreams of freedom, mixing them with the salt. As the experience of Slavery cuts into the skin of the slaves, it also cuts into the consciousnesses and lives of their descendants and may receive succor through Jack's "rememory"[40] and Sekou's "re member meant."[41] It is *Mothernation's* "pelican song": it turns "our saltblasted backs / to mirror the sun"; it is Sekou, extending his aesthetics of salt (and political solidarity) beyond St. Martin with "report from the country," denouncing dictators who "bleed the salt of the land" and in "caribbean civilization," chanting revolution in "a corridor of sea salt and blood."

Extending Sekou's aesthetics beyond St. Martin brings us to an encounter with sugar (and cotton), the salt of others, especially in the Caribbean and the Americas. According to *The Salt Reaper's* "tortured fragments," the salt-picking, the cane cutting (and the picking of cotton) in Slavery and the subsequent forms and experiences of labor—and political—exploitation and oppression, left scars, cuts, and corns on the physical skin and Brathwaitian psyche of the people, on the soul of the place:

> sssssssssssssssssssssssssssinging ship of the
> watersea&bloodtear
> sssssssssssssssssssssssssssinging field of the
> canecut&cottonred
> shhhhhhhhhhhhhhhhhhhear of skin
> sssssssssssssssssssssssssseared open
> &corned with pond plots of salt

This poem has of course a far more global and contemporary reach than might be thought from the above lines alone. In fact, it concludes with references to the Jewish Holocaust and the Palestinian Intifada, linked in an alarming "knotted memory." However, this excerpt also allows us to understand the aspect that pain bears in the poet's salt-related works.

The great pain of Slavery, becoming, laying claim, and the ongoing fight for freedom, justice, and liberation of the new nation(s), X/Self, and i&i, form and reform in the works of Sekou on salt; this all is found in an instance, in *Mothernation's* "the house we are building." Here, the poetic voice appears, calling on all those who "could tenant this body,"[42] drawing in the descendants of the indigenous, enslaved, indentured, settlers, slavers, colonizers, and immigrants: "we have here / plowed stakes in this new world earth / made fertile with sweat / [...] chained through the ages of cane / [...] wading through a saga of brine / picking harvests of salt."[43] In these lines, embracing shared legacies and incorporating both the sweat of salt and the pain of the cane cutters, sugar and salt appear again. All of this pain is depicted again by Sekou.

The Martinican scholar and artist Patricia Donatien-Yssa recognized all of these expressions of pain in the works of Caribbean poets what she defined as "exorcisme de la blès."[44] In her comparative analysis of Caribbean writers and painters, she develops an "aesthetics of the pain and suffering" that emerges out of centuries of Slavery and violence, and which she herself derived from *Antilles déjà jadis* (1999), by the Martinican scholar René Ménil.

This aesthetics of the pain also marks Sekou's poetry and fiction. Although he is not a painter, his collections of writing are often oriented toward pictures, drawings, works of the visual arts, and videos, beginning with his first published poetry collections. Sekou is a visive artist: his way of depicting in writing is realistic and vivid; it oozes with hues of a palette filled with centuries-old pain, like these singing lines in *Mothernation's* "easter sunday": "This Sunday / robed in purple and black / wrapped in pinks and marooned / fleshes and bloods." In Sekou, the aggressiveness of the denunciation of the brutality of Slavery, the mask of exploitation today, and the intention to shape a new consciousness, a new country alternately growing, being toned down by the sweet nostalgia of be/longing, as in the *Quimbé* poem "4": "a tear of pain / is a pillow of salt tending our wound of longing." This affective disorder of the poet finds a mirror image in Clarke's expression of poetics: "Eye write; Eye paint; Eye sing! Eye confess to be possessed by a malady."[45] This malady, the sensitivity that belongs to the finest poets, is the purple tone in the rough colors of be/longing and the past, washed away by the salty waters of a new shore, as in the novella on the child charge of Nana Mandisa.

Sekou's island holds a new beginning, soaked in a painful past. His nostalgic tones are memories of a centennial motherland, whose salt waters in its salt pond are its essence, in Kristeva's "thetic phase." In this conflict between Same and Other, what Glissant calls *Même* and *Divers*, a poetic inlay appears: the written becomes a calque, a cast, of the oral, shadowing aspects of the preceding culture, as in his *Le discours antillais*. Sekou's contribution to

St. Martin's national culture includes the fact that the people of St. Martin can recognize the duality of their cultural and literary productions, especially where the poet echoes the national dance *ponum* and the song *quimbé*, as these are remembered in *Fête—Celebrating The Traditional Festive Music of St. Martin* (1992) and *Fête—Celebrating St. Martin's Traditional Festive Music—Revised Edition* (2008). In this reservoir of suffering, a salty gloss is deposited on the poet's writing, leaving desolation and a longing for a previously suffered past, or in Glissant's poetic expression, a dried "salt of death" in *Le discours antillais*, covering up the suffering:

> Quand nous vaquons, quelque chose se détache quelque part, d'une souffrance, d'un cri, et se dépose en nous. Le sel de mort sur le troupeaux taris, au travers d'un désert nomade qui n'est certes pas liberté.

Early grains: symbols of the woman, the land, the salt

Sekou's first work was the collection *Moods for Isis—Picture poems of Love & Struggle*. It was named after a girlfriend from high school in New York City, the site where the poems were written, and where Sekou had migrated to from St. Martin in 1972. The book was self-published in 1978. Isis, of course, is the name of a goddess of Ancient Egypt, who governed fertility, the divine wife and mother goddess. Given the permeating "Afrikan" theme and the steady depiction of women, sacred and profane, this is the aspect of the name that probably serves as the more relevant part of the backdrop and what indicates its moods.

In *Moods for Isis* the woman is equally idolized and condemned but mostly veneered as her figure is dissected into its several layers, mother (and motherland), sister, friend, lover, and/or prostitute. She cathects and invests as much of herself in building relationships as in building a better nation, through work, pain, and endurance. Men are depicted in this debut volume as warriors, workers, and fathers as well as people stuck in a "bar room," as in the poem "Untitled," or as a "bastard" in the short verse "Denunciation." The teenage poet's wrath spares neither women nor men.

Whether for political reasons or from a thirst for social justice, the poems in this collection bear screams demanding equality or are raised to the sky to question the works of god or the devil (oriented toward different beliefs, animist, Christian, or Islamic) regarding the injustices we experience on earth.

Among these, the proportion between libertine love or prostitution is out of balance with the sacredness of maternity: the power of sex is intertwined with the womb and its desecration. These two elements point at the counterposition between salt and sugar, which we witness in the "salty rings around their eyes" from "Call Upon Triumph," which are the antithesis of the "sweet wines" in "Freeze."

The sad laborer in "Rock of Ages" is asked for the reason of his gloom: is it that he never reaped what he sowed—referring to Galatians 6—or has he poured his "tears and sweet sweat water" onto the land he was working? His salty tears and sweat are fluids from the body, fertilizing and nourishing or polluting the land, which is both earth and woman. In "A Kwanza Poem," the Black man is exhorted to be "the planter of the seed / that impregnates the earth." This poem carries a small freight of political propaganda, as Fergus argues in *Love Labor Liberation in Lasana Sekou*: "The lines speak not of seminal planting, but the propagation of revolutionary ideas." Growing crops changes from a purely physical act and becomes deeply spiritual or progressively political, in that the seeds of poetic enthusiasm feed the womb and the children, and "maternity" acquires a higher purpose as we shift our perception of the mother from an individual to a collective, such as food and hunger expand their primary meaning in poems like "Holocaust," "When Hungry," or "Weeping."

In *Moods for Isis*, words are accompanied by drawings and photographs of fists exhorting battle, a fetus in the teardrop of a woman, or images of gods or haunting shadows. These are meant to urge people to enhance their selves and do battle to improve society in all ways possible. Society can improve when everyone is aware that it needs to improve and will thus adopt this urgency into their own selves. The betterment of the self is a prompt and an answer to the need for a change: when each individual feels a need to improve and then improves him- or herself, then all society will be improved. In this way, society will feel free because it will be made up of enlightened individuals. These themes are pivotal for the spirit of freedom, hinging on the wish to escape, such as in the ancestral act of *marronage*, as in the poems "Our Time" and "Then."

Sekou reminds us that sometimes, we must go back to grow or improve, embracing our origins, like the poet of war does (Sekou refers to himself with this term "P.O.W. [Poets of War]"). After such a return, the poet becomes empowered with a consciousness that can call upon others to break free and become fed with nutrients of the "Self." Much work needs to be done, to help those such as the "scattered and disillusioned" children of Africa all over the "'Western' places" in the poem "Oh Afrikaland," suffering from the monetary enslavement they are shackled to. The idea that we can nourish our souls and minds so that oppressed or struggling people can survive and gain in strength returns again and again in *Moods for Isis*.

In this collection, blood saturates many poems, giving them the aspect of old wounds that have not healed and are still bleeding, wounds given by colonization and Slavery and by the hard and exploitative work in the fields from the scattering of a people all over the world against their will, or by the cut of the "(umbilical) cord," which was torn at the moment of deportation. However, the amputation of the cord also occurs in a new birth, and in Sekou's *Moods for Isis* we can hear, beyond desperation and the sense of the oppression in the historical past, hope and an impetus toward a new future, where a new identity will be created that can bring old and the new together. This may be the new face of the USA (whose Black American struggle the poet identifies with and where he will live and study until 1984), Africa (the poet is influenced here by significant Black American poets and historians of the day), the Caribbean (influenced by progressive kaiso and reggae singers and echoes of the St. Martin he migrated from in 1972) a creolized, or, in modern terms, a globalized image.

The grains of the symbols that Sekou uses consistently in repeated re-elaborations in his work appear here. The woman, the land, freedom, the nourishment and pain of sweet and salty substances, youth, Africa, Rastafari, political independence, revolution, and improvement of the self are critical elements in his themes of love, labor, and liberation. They continuously fertilize his aesthetics of salt, emanating from the sea and the Great Salt Pond. They are scattered about, ready for planting in fertile fields, or they are already in focus in *Moods for Isis*.

Salty lives of some island women

The themes, the presence of salt, and the concept of *marronage* in modern times are present from the very beginning of Sekou's work, for both male and female protagonists. It is also intriguing to consider how the author relates the features of salt and marronage both symbolically and realistically to woman or to what woman represents, either in society or to Sekou, spiritually, psychologically, romantically, and historically. Overall, however, in Sekou's *Love Songs Make You Cry* (1989) his characters and their actions are considered separately in the different short stories, albeit linked by a subtle red thread, which orients their actions in similar ways, despite their life situations, which are completely at variance.

The five stories in *Love Songs Make You Cry* dramatically illustrate the lives of people in St. Martin. Multiple topics surface: immigration, prostitution, mental illness, and witchcraft or Obeah in "The Snoring," to love, betrayal, and forgiveness in "Fatty and the Big House"; from a sick love that crosses boundaries and countries to family love in "New Year's Eve Birth," politics and heritage in "The Rightful Heirs," and finally the idea of the love song in the title story, "Love Songs Make You Cry."

Salt clearly appears in "The Snoring"—the lead character Elsa learns that she is expecting a child and "craved salty foods," she also experiences "feeling sick all the time, gettin' all mahga n'ting." The Rastaman who helps to care for her at Dolores's place brings her instead "Ital" food, which is "saltless." Elsa and the woman of the "shack" where the sixteen-year-old is hiding and being cared for in the village of Middle Region are the means through which the idea of contemporary *marronage* is introduced. Dolores lives and works at night, dealing with "clients," but she also expresses her deep sense of humanity in helping Elsa. The reader recognizes that Sekou's glance is here reaching beyond the surface and into the depths of the human being, illustrating a means of perception that is capable of scratching off the surface of social stigma and recognizing the good in people's hearts. This may be Dolores's way of redeeming herself or a recognition of some traits in common with Elsa.

The characters of Elsa, a St. Martin teenager, and Dolores, who is from the Dominican Republic, may have brought them together because of their common state as "refugees," bringing forth a theme that has not lost its urgency and poignancy today, as we witness millions of refugees escaping war zones and heading to Europe. Under the dim light in her shack, with Elsa looking on, Dolores,

> while dressing for work, moved under the naked bulb light and showed her guest the maroon scars and some of the still healing scratches on her thighs and belly she got from running through the hills late at night to escape the immigration raids.

Elsa is trying to escape from a dangerous relationship: she is pregnant by Wilfred, an older, important businessman who is married and does not love her. She is also escaping from her grandmother, who is very poor, beats her, and sharply criticizes her for being in a relationship with Wilfred, for "let'n man ruin yo' body." Dazed, at the end of her wandering that began that fated early morning, when she was chased angrily from Granny's house and Wilfred's office, she is approached by Dolores as she is returning from her work. In this way, in their genuine sisterhood and sororal affection, Elsa "loved the warriorwoman returning each morning."

Sekou's interweaving of spoken creoles throughout his writing is a marker of the peculiar linguistic situation that prevails on St. Martin. In his review of this book in *The Caribbean Writer*, Fergus adds that "The stories are scant of dialogue but the author reveals character by using the idiom of his people in his narrative."[46] All of this is reflected immediately at the beginning in "The Snoring" and in the other stories as well. Sekou also weaves French and Spanish words and expressions in naturally, fitting them into what Daniella Jeffry called in her introduction to the collection "the island's vernacular" or "'Afro-New World' English."

In "Fatty and the Big House," the second story in *Love Songs Make You Cry*, the idea of salt is more closely intertwined with bodily fluids. The title character Fatty, oppressed with the idea that his wife

Annie is cheating on him, as insinuated to him by a gossiping woman, enters into a metaphorical "salt pond of shame that gurgled around him somehow like a pool of blood." When Fatty catches Annie red handed in the act of wronging him, he begins to ooze salty bodily fluids: "sweat and tears salted his eyes." However, after both have fled the island in shame, Fatty and Annie are re-united and return home with their children. As the plane approaches the island,

> He held his beloved's hand, and she rested her head on his chest.
> Fatty looked over at his children and was filled with great joy and fatherly pride. He smiled warmly at the children's excitement as they peered out of the plane's window to at last set eyes on his "sweet S'maatin".

The third story is the greatest locus of salt references in the book, which climax when Clement is being approached by a hitman, engaged by the father of his ex-lover, Blair, to kill him. Clement is awoken with a bucket of saltwater, and he feels "powder grains of salt that spiked the lids of his eyes." Salt is here associated with pain. However Clement, a warrior and a political independentist, loyal to the "Committee of S'maatiners" who has sworn "The Oath of Soualiga," here fights even on the brink of death, "fighting even now for the living of his people by not betraying another flowering of their struggle to wrestle from any form of oppression their free and Independent future." This maroon spirit also surfaces in Clement's words of resistance, "of an ancient and eternal manhood that had survived even the limbo ordeal of the Middle Passage." As Clement and Blair are linked in a destiny of death, as Clement's body is dumped into the "fertile" Caribbean Sea, Blair commits suicide by overdosing on drugs, and she drowns in the waters where they made love as teenagers.

Here, the salty sea is for Sekou the recipient of both life and death. This sea, with its currents, ebbs, and flows, exhibits a kind of positivity, perhaps because it is linked to Mother Africa, the "Afrique" spoken of in *Moods for Isis* in the poem "In Time," where the poet expresses a longing to spiritually "journey back" to it.

In the fourth story, the presence of an old European family, who supposedly have a claim to being the rightful heirs to St. Martin, undermines the foundation of the 1648 Treaty of Concordia. This still-powerful family is working to regain possession. Their work lies behind the deaths of Mr. Richards and Taata, "s'maatin heroes and freedom fighters." Much political commitment appears in the background of this short story, which incites the reader to S'maatinize the island and make of it a rightful and just society. Freedom fighters from the time of Slavery are added to a list of other underground warriors:

> Thomas Duruo, who taught the people about Marcus Garvey and pride in theyself; Jose Lake, Sr. who wrote in his newspaper and spoke out for our rights when nobody else would; and Alrett Peters, who was a first union man.

"The Rightful Heirs" ends with an undated extract from the journal of the wise Flavius. His words are directed toward "all the youths who come like pilgrims to these old steps" and can complete their pilgrimage only if they fight for their land, as it is said "by the sweat and blood and tears of our forebears." Once more, salty bodily fluids are symbolically and critically associated with a history of pain and sacrifice, of Slavery and terror. How can the people of St. Martin now, in the present be deprived of all this because of the colonial lineage of people with no relationship to the island? Sekou allows the aged Flavius to have the last words, where St. Martin land is epitomized into a woman, as if he is speaking for both the present and the future Flavius:

> I tell these youths to better lay claim, ... it's our heritage. All you better know it's going to be a fight to keep her. St. Martin is like a fresh and beautiful country girl, and all the rich and powerful suitors coming here from all around want to use her for themselves. But we are the rightful heirs.

The fifth and last story of the collection, "Love Songs Make You Cry," narrates a young woman and a young man who are slowly falling in love in Carnival Village—"at this time, settled on a spread of 'landfill' anchored out into the pond." A somewhat seamy intersection appears between the love that the young woman's lover provides and the money she receives from another man. Her attitude toward struggle is the interesting point for our discussion here. She is a hairdresser, and she is more openly political than the women of the preceding stories. She discusses local and regional issues with her lover (neither of the two young people are given names in the story): race, Maurice Bishop, Fidel Castro, ideology and "Caribbean nationhood," "radical women," whether independence is possible for "San Martin," governmental corruption, and "the systems keeping us down." Regarding immigration, "she hated the raids."

"I would never run. Why? And scratch up my legs and belly with the barbed wire in the hills? Where are they taking me when they catch me? They are sending me back to my country." She would look at him, stroke his brow. "Like you, I love my country. I am not ashamed of my country."

While this is a love story, the politics that is interwoven with it, even if it is somewhat overly controlled by the author's voice, as Fergus warns us, draws us in with a vicarious concern into the central business of Sekou's ideas and the symbols of *marronage* in our times.

If the maroon element existed in the spirit of escape and survival for Elsa and Dolores in the opening of "Love Songs Make You Cry," then the book ends at the symbolic peak of a consciousness of the construction of a maroon nation. In the words of the young woman (uttered by her to explain why she is returning home):

> [I]f I am a fighting woman, a woman with knowledge, working with a people's movement for some change, I and my child will be better off in Santo Domingo. You know, yes, that in the Caribbean our success, our new system must come though, from what you call our, our own genius.

> Shouldn't we stop this mimicking left, right and center? All that has failed us. And isn't that why your Bishop was killed by traitors?

In his *Sovereignty of the Imagination* (2009), Lamming asserts that, "The Caribbean is our own experiment in a unique expression of human civilisation." This is true in many ways, whether in pure or in an admixed ways among the region's people as a whole, whether for its ethnic groups, for its writers and artists, and for its men and women, all equally. In *Love Songs Make You Cry*, the author of the narratives and the characters in them confirm this dynamic position: "Sekou, as in his poetry, is searching for his own form in the story," Fergus notes.[47] The lives of the island women in this first St. Martin collection of short stories marks the passage from salty lives to embodiments of marronage.

THE CREOLE ABENG:
MARRONAGE IN SEKOU'S POETRY

> *If you allow yourself
> to forget the sound of your town's horn,
> you get lost in the gathering.*
>
> – Akan proverb, Ghana

Because no one can be justified in imprisoning, torturing, buying and selling, or in forcing men and women to perform hard labor in chains in their thirst for power and the false belief than one race is superior to another, then *marronage* is not a crime. Nonetheless, it was punished as such, because, as we know, universal truths and human law reside in different dimensions.

Marronage, a borrowing of the French *marronage*, is an act derived from the thirst for freedom and as an act of resistance against the abuses and injustices of Slavery, was probably born together with Slavery itself. However, the word itself only began to be used after 1500. The enslaved people who ran away from plantations in the Caribbean and the Americas to find refuge in the woods, swamps, or in the hills or mountains were called *cimarrón* by the Spanish, a derivative of the word *cima*, meaning the top of hills or mountains where maroons escaped to. We are reminded by Gabriel Debien of the origin of the word *marron*, probably derived from the name of the tribe Symarons.[48] The causes of the flight of escaped slaves are not limited to the will to be free, testified by Père Du Tertre in the seventeenth century with regard to French colonies,[49] but affliction and want played a part as well, such as in the lack of food and the inhuman conditions and punishments, especially for enslaved people who could not or refused to work and obey the slave drivers. The tensions arising within the ecosystem of the plantation could result in the murder of a plantation supervisor, who was called the *gérant* or the *économe* in the French colonies.[50]

Rochmann examines the phenomenon of *marronage* in its relationship to Slavery and to *marron bossale* (African-born) and *creoles*, arguing that it was born at a certain time and stopped after it was suppressed. As she notes, *marronage* came to prominence after the spread of independence that began in the early 1800s (Haitian independence and abolitionism in England, in the US, and in France. Myths about figures like Nanny in Jamaica, a maroon leader and considered to have Obeah (spiritual or healing) powers, arose as well. Rochmann retrieves the peculiar presence of maroons in novels, noting chronological jumps in their narratives, which reproduce the evasions of the maroons during their rise in the hills and mountains.[51] Even though this could be seen as a stylistic choice that underlines a lack of historical certainty or documentation, in which the writing may fail when it is entrusted only to memory. She identifies the maroon aesthetics as exhibiting a "renoncement á l'idéologie du territoire,"[52] but this does not apply to Sekou's poetry, as he imbricates the maroons within the territory and the "I-lands,"[53] and as he sings in the poem "All Labor" from *Maroon Lives* (1983, 2014): "We labored / In the tradition of maroons / And grew / […] / On this Caribbean isle we stood / One with water and land and sky / One people." If we extended the concept to encompass all human beings who resist abuse or the negative aspects of colonial experience, then we can argue that maroons still exist today. They are indeed present in Sekou's poetry and in his narratives.

Sekou's vision of the figure of the maroon includes maroon silos, *quilombos*, *mocambos*, *palenqueros*, and all the various names used to refer to the historical maroons, and to the maroon nations of the Caribbean and the Americas that are known to us. The *quilombos* are the Brazilian maroons, and Sekou mentions them in the *Maroon Lives* poem "For Walter Rodney" that he dedicated to the great Guyanese anti-capitalist who was assassinated in 1980: to "Organize there / In the camps of Accabre"; Accabre was a leader of the 1763 slave revolt against the Dutch in Guyana. The *quilombo* and *mocambo*, maroon settlements in Brazil, are mentioned also at the end of the long poem "Nativity," where Sekou puts forth an appeal to maroons in different mountain ranges and settlements, villages, and nations of the Caribbean and the Americas.

In her introduction to *Nativity and monologues for today*, Napolina Gumbs remarks that to Sekou: "The people, at their best, are guerrilla fighters (maroon silos) who have never surrendered." This is underlined in the following lines from the poem "Nativity": "pelican hearts / & / lion gaits are maroon silos / sailing & stalking / through windstorms' burn / toil & tossed around / but steady rudders ready we." Here the pelican (the national bird of St. Martin) becomes, like the lion, a symbol of strength or the lion's gait (the stride of the Rastafarian), an embodiment of the maroon fighters and of the survivors, as well as an emblem for younger St. Martiners, for Caribbean youth, and for the youth of the Americas.

In the first edition of *Nativity* and in *Nativity / Nativité / Natividad—Trilingual Edition* (2010), references to Black Jacobins remind us of C.L.R. James's text on the legendary Haitian Revolution. This reminder recalls the memory of Toussaint L'Ouverture, who fought against the plantocracy and colonists to free Saint-Domingue and who worked to implement a new political and economic regime for this country but died in France the year before the declaration of independence by Jean-Jacques Dessalines. Later in the poem, Sekou takes us "up river / where I Sought My Brother / & love maroons who never sign to treaty / dey self away." The maroons are "up river" and on the hills: "but the hills / it is true / are again pregnant from our *rammagé* / & meh son […] / we are / all & the same / Acabre, / Delgres, Fedon, Dessalines." The word *rammagé* that Sekou uses in this passage may refer to the chirping of birds, here describing the free maroons, communicating in the hills, and becoming a reference to the sound of the contemporary steel band.[54]

In the book *For The Mighty Gods*, the maroons appear in the poem "Sunspice." This poem unfolds with love and passion, telling of a man/an explorer/ or perhaps the poet himself who is climbing into the hills and mountains of an island he is trying to conquer, depicted as a man making love to a woman. Here, love is an expression of nationalist love and dedication, of curiosity in experiencing and conquering, along with the transcendence of physical boundaries. In the poem "crimson cross" from *Quimbé*, such boundaries allow no hiding place: "and even in the hills / there will be no rock under which to hide," but in "older heads," this ascension is understood as a means of developing spiritual improvement, a sort of renewal, as with family: "it is a time of blessing / to ascend the bluestone hills." This sense of blessing and communion with nature and spirituality had been given expanded expression in *Mothernation*, in the work "visit jamaica," where the heights of the Cockpit country provide a secluded environment and preserve the history of the maroons:

> to reap a millennial harvest of light
> that flourishes hidden
> in the maroon cradle of cockpit ites.

Mothernation contains references to maroons throughout. In "lendépandans," they appear in the call for "more more mo' *ma ma maronage*." This surging line is inextricably linked to the land: the body of the maroon is the body of the island itself. This poem supporting the independence movement speaks of "gwadloupe"; it was recited by Sekou on Radio Tanbou on his first visit to the island of Guadeloupe in 1987—invited by the teachers of English association to read his poetry at a meeting of its members. The links of land, love, and escape in *marronage*, forming a celebration of a continuing phenomenon or as modernized symbol in Sekou's poetry reaches an emotional climax in the poem "on raids," where "'we spent the night in the hills last night. / running from the immigration' / trodding nights / pacing the hills." In "jhennie," a poem of romance and solidarity, a woman is again depicted as being on the run from immigration:

> could you have known
> that my land
> our caribbean land
> would cage your body
> and that i would meet you
> here, on the run?
> and that we would ka-danse
> into each other's arms

A reading of "caribbean journey," with its labor- and culture-fueled, surging style, shows Sekou's mixing of names of artists working in popular culture or of their works, with an effect that is similar to the one he achieves with the use of literary and scholarly works and authors, whether well known or obscure, along with revolutionary figures and historical places and events and the names and deeds of national or local heroes. For instance, he includes a reference to the Martinican Joseph Zobel's movie *La Rue Cases-Nègres*. This reference carries a double-meaning and is also a reminder, introducing memory or awareness of what is named, or a new function of association with the subject matter. This effect resembles James's *Black Jacobins*, present in "Nativity." Here, the title of Zobel's movie appears, without upsetting the *flow* or *riddim* in any way in its relationship to the complex of interconnected and contextualized names and images of salt, sugar, landscapes, culture, maroons, liberators, and others:

> down sugarcane alleys
> we coming
> down the Black shack alleys
> across the saltponds and pondfills
> across the valleys, soothing savannas
> and down the hillsides / we coming
> up through the cotton field and coal keels
> the banana groves and bauxite mines (...)
>
> to people the maroon lands
> to plow-share up the sierra maestra ites
> to find refuge and renewal

in the facial mangroves of the beloved bearded ones
in the life-cleansing blood of the she-saviors.

This form of association reminds us of our interconnectedness and can also unearth and introduce new, authentic memories and meanings in the text or in other forms or genres presented, and it serves in no small measure to bring out the substance and style that identifies Sekou's poetry. In his authoritative, boundaries-crossing introduction to *Corazón de Pelícano / Pelican Heart* (2010), a bilingual anthology of Sekou's poems, Rodríguez defines this technique, in its use by Sekou, using examples of its appearance in the poem "pelican song" from *Mothernation*:

> Caribbean intertextual conversation increases, whether with interpolated/appropriated quotations... or with the inclusion of a title, winking at both the author and the reader, like a crouching stowaway, in the middle of a line, or a double pun of homophonous words associating their meaning with the names of local or regional historic or cultural figures, such as the allusions to journalist and politician Joseph Lake, Sr. and theologian and essayist Armando Lampe: "who are we now / who will swell like a lake / to flood the tyrants / and with us water our fields / to shatter the deafening darkness / like the lighted voice of a 'lampe'?"

The title of *Maroon Lives—for Grenadian freedom fighters* (1983) itself underlines the importance of the theme of *marronage*. The rage that lingers at the foundation of these poems is expressed in the prefatory poem "Rally Round": "The rebels are still in the fields." By rallying the maroons or the maroon spirit or idea in the failure of the Grenada Revolution, Sekou refers to "constant *images in the yard*," his own poetry collection published that same year. This title is inserted within a stanza-long list of names of texts and musical recordings, all camouflaged, in a pre-"Nativity" technique of association:

> We remain
> The sweat of the first morning dew
> Grains of wheat
> Arrows of living gods
> Constant images in the yard
> Confirmations
> Conspiracies of dark old men
> Uprisings
> On the route to revolution
> In the tradition of always readiness
> Rising from ashes and embers
> Like winds above the hills
> *Siempre*, returning to the source

The theme of *marronage* is expressed again in the lines of the last stanza: "I tell you / Behind the mountains /

Are mountains growing." In "Re-organize" he invites the children and young to arm for fighting and "to the maroons." Similarly in "Resistance," the maroons become "nation-builders," fighters for independence, and following the historical idea that has descended to us of the maroons, Sekou spurs the reader toward a secret combat of runaways: "We will stay in the hills then / And grow strong as baobab trees / Stay underground / And run deep as eternal roots." The title verse, "Maroon Lives," is dedicated to marronage and brings out Rastafarian tones, inviting "workers and warriors" to "Defy the Babylonian whore / And its wuthless minions / Who defile our land" and seek to "trample" those who "labored / In these fields."

Language itself, in this collection, is being used as an abeng, more than in any other of Sekou's books of poetry before this point. This is most visible in "We Continue," found in the second of the book's three thematic sections. Badejo draws the following conclusions on this work:

> It is an inexorable march to victory, especially if nurtured by love and labor. If "The Triumphant Living" is an indictment of imperialism and "The Greatest March" an anthem of certain victory, "We Continue" is a hymn to Pan-Caribbean unity and hemispheric brotherhood. This "bilingual poem" is

without doubt, the most successful in this section. It is also the poem that most lyrically reflects Sekou's vision of the Caribbean. In content and in style, the thrust here is toward Caribbean integration.[55]

In Badejo's "Revolution as Poetic Inspiration: Grenada in 'Maroon Lives' by Lasana Sekou" (1984), the revolutionary spirit that lies underneath the surface of Sekou's fourth collection is underscored. His anti-imperialization and anti-balkanization ideology guide his attacks on US foreign policy and politics, and his stand "with the leftist revolutions in Africa, Latin America and the Caribbean" are highlighted by Badejo in that paper, first delivered at the Ninth Annual Conference of the Caribbean Studies Association. Badejo's critical essay has been published in one volume with all of the poems in Sekou's collection in the second edition of *Maroon Lives* (2014). The work of Sekou and Badejo in *Maroon Lives* has since been referenced by the United States Military Academy associate professor John C. Nelson in "A 'Parvenu Predator'? When the Kill Zone and the Contact Zone Collide on the Isle of Spice," his chapter from *Caribbean Military Encounters* (2017).

Thirty years after *Maroon Lives* was first published in New York City, and within weeks of the murder of Prime Minister Maurice Bishop by a member of an opposing faction of his revolutionary government, followed by the US-led invasion of the Spice Isle, University of Toronto professor Keith Ellis remarks in his discussion, printed in the title's new edition, that the "supple, integrative language, engaging scholarship, expansive allusions, sharp wit, musical vigor at the command of Lasana M. Sekou, make *Maroon Lives* resonate with other times and places." However much Sekou's poetry can emerge in this collection as an expression of rage and saturated with invective, space remains for hope to dwell that a unified, just society can be developed.

Sekou's body of literature, and especially *Maroon Lives*, expresses the hope that people will become free from the shackles of every kind of slavery—racism, lack of education or employment, diseases, corruption; and as Badejo puts it, "The poet is marching with the masses, not on horseback, but on foot, like a maroon in the hills."

St. Martin: colonial or postcolonial?

It is still an open question whether contemporary St. Martin can be considered a postcolonial society. Must such a society be completely free from colonial domination and influence, or can it be still attached by its navel string to its former colonizing power, with the burden of having to deal with new global socioeconomic issues that maintain their influence?

In the way that Sekou is inclined toward freedom and liberation for his island or *mothernation*, so too is his brother, Joseph H. Lake, Jr., who published an interesting article in *The Independence Papers, Volume 1* (1990), a collection of political pamphlets, essays, and newspaper articles which is intended to move the political conscience of the people of St. Martin to prepare for and embrace independence. This article has a provocative and aggressive tone, but it is aimed at awakening the conscience of St. Martin. Lake maintains that "Plantation St. Maarten 1788" is no different from "Plantation St. Maarten 1988." Thus, this political scientist and journalist argues that, to make progress and become independent, "Plantation St. Maarten must be totally destroyed" to give way to a new society, as the old (colonial) and the new (independent) cannot coexist.

Dr. Rhoda Arrindell, in the introduction to this volume, handed the baton over to an array of writers, all focusing on St. Martin's political status and its need for a *status aparte* or independence. In particular, Sekou remarked on the fundamental role of artists in his article "The Artists' Role on the Road Towards Independence for St. Maarten." The poet called on the island's artists and cultural workers to create a common battlefield, expressed in their works, to ensure that the people will not feel abandoned in the political struggle. He generally maintains that people from every corner of society must become involved in the struggle for political independence. In his essay "A National Youth Agenda on Independence: Teachers' Role in Preparing Youths for Independence," Sekou writes that young people "are of primary and critical importance to the success of a nation's Independence."

The importance of youth and artists to a society, their foundational role in building a nation, is a focus in Sekou's long poem "The cubs are in the field," from his chapbook *Big Up St. Martin: Essay & Poem* (1999). Sekou recognizes that to construct a nation, you need national symbols, as recognized by his *National Symbols of St. Martin*. Among these symbols in *Big Up St. Martin* are the inhabitants of St. Martin as cubs, the children of the lion, maroons, determined to survive in the fields, courageous, proud of their own, their land, their island, their motherland, and their country. In this poem, ready to suffer, organize, fight, and defend to build a "flourishing" nation,

> try they will, to maraud thy birthright of sweet land.
> but you are the cubs in the field
> the long time is your catacomb lair
> your ticket of maroon massif
> forge & refuge for our restless rage
> washes the wanna-be weave from the hair
> of runaways to the field

"The cubs are in the field" is a song of the construction and proud maintenance of the sweet land of St. Martin, which belongs to the cubs, not to the colonizing hunters or anyone else who may try to take it away. The land echoes in its sanctity as a catacomb of centuries of enslavement, and it becomes a woven fabric that forms the cubs' lair, punctuated by maroons. Like the maroons communicated with the *abeng* and blew the call to battle on this horn made of shell, so Sekou makes his poem echo with names of national artists and youths, as sacred as the names recited in a rosary:

> telling tales from the great salt pond
> showering in rainy seasons
> tuning the sweet salt of songs
> ehm... ehm... ehm...
> okay, esther
> okay, debbie
> okay, miguel
> okay, vanessa

okay, angelo
okay, jean baptiste
okay, dominga
okay, priya
okay, wang cheung
okay, kwame...
the cubs are in the field

The names of the St. Martin artists and everyday people of a range of heritages that appear here are appealed to for their testimony to the importance of the arts in and for St. Martin and to unite their artistic and spiritual strength to build the nation. The first three names called in the above excerpt, are those of poet Esther Gumbs, poet and artist Drisana Deborah Jack, and digital artist Angelo Rombley. When it is read or heard, "The cubs in the field" reminds the hearer of the *ponum* song, preserving the memories of the salt ponds and the runaway cubs in the fields. The artists are here being marshaled in the fields to preserve the memory of the nation. The conservation of memory and tradition is important too as a nation is built, and for this reason, the *ponum* song echoes in the hills, valleys, and on the pond: "telling tales from the great salt pond / showering in rainy seasons / tuning the sweet salt of songs."

The search for national symbols that can unify and function as a means of identification and unification also emerges from the essay "Colony, Territory, or Partner?" in the same *Big Up St. Martin*. Functioning as a political overview of the state of the Netherlands Antilles at the time, this essay deals with the political reality of the "island territories" that make up the Antilles and their lack of any

> unifying cultural symbols beyond those resilient linking national symbols of every Caribbean nation that through history, marronage, liberation struggles, family, geography, cultural arts, labor and trade continue to bond the archipelago, not as one country, but certainly with clearly defined and dynamic variables identifying us as the Caribbean People.

It is reinforced once again:

> The Netherlands Antilles, a colonial construct, and Antillean Day celebrate, not people, not a shared culture, or the resilient linking national symbols of our Caribbean but… colonialism.

As an artist, Sekou knew and still knows that it is important to insist on cultural identification, and again, on national symbols, and on self-pride, to recognize the fact that St. Martin has much to offer and is able to sustain itself, despite its small size in the sense of territory. Along the road he is traveling to independence, Sekou relies on the cultural function and historical role of the maroons, who fought for freedom and must be considered a lighthouse and an inspirational beacon guiding toward democratization:

> the "bold and brave" tradition and freedom fighters dotting our political culture must now be held up as shining examples of our continuing struggle for true people's democracy on St. Martin.

"Resistance Nation" and a theory of the "village chiefs"

In "maroon nation" in *Quimbé*, the range of the political address is no longer local but has become glocal, with references to Haiti, Jamaica, Argentina, and the US, calling most of all to Sekou's idea of the village chiefs and the maroons in the island's past, whom we will consider after reading an extract of the poem:

> Caribbean manhood
> is maroon
> it's not noreiga [Noriega, NbR]
> nothing like argentinian generals [...]
> Caribbean manhood
> is nothing like ton'ton macoutes [...]

> when *imperialista* come down from ill *norte* [...]
> Caribbean manhood
> is not constructed in caribbean schools
> 'causin it is maroon
> and offends babylon system [...]
> because it belongs to runaways
> who can't be controlled by whips
> and petty village chiefs who always catching cold
> from a fart of wind blown from afar
> where they believe better always come from
> so da's woi so much ah we always so sicky sicky [...]
>
> Caribbean manhood
> is *cimarron* family is *marronage* nation is
> maroon colored
> civilization borning [...]
> see how maroon caribbean manhood is out there [...]
> warriors down from the hills
> battling your roof from dusk to dawn
> to disturb your slavery
> make you grow up to damn well know
> what is going on to save your life

This poem is political. It is saturated with references to the maroons, to the spirit of resistance, and to Sekou's theory of the village chief. There is a genuine warrior nature to be found within or among the Caribbean people, according to Sekou, as evident in their maroon history. Local, indigenous matters should be prioritized by local chiefs/politicians, who instead, Sekou laments, are more concerned with extraneous political matters, between the polity and their current or former colonizers or the imperialistic politics of the US, "when *imperialista* come down from ill *norte*." The poet is very critical of US imperialist politics. He describes them with the blanket term "ill *norte*," a distortion of the Spanish phrase *el norte*, the north, punning on the ill work in reference to characterizing the association of local politics with the US by the "petty village chiefs who always catching cold," exploiting the difference in climate between the Caribbean and the northern mainland in service of this image.

Sekou seems to be bringing a profound criticism to bear on the pettiness of these village chiefs, with their xenophilia and narrow-minded treatment of local or national political matters. These politricksters, in a phrase that he uses, are more open to what is outside than toward what is inside because they look to outer forces, "where they believe better always come from" and "so da's woi so much ah we always so sicky sicky," extending this image of poor health to the political, social, and economic situation and to the spiritual lack of ease among the people. In "maroon nation," the maroon is treated as a hero with Rastafarian overtones, characterize with both *marronage* and Rastafarian goal to "offend[...] Babylon system." Maroons, runaways, fighting for their freedom, acting independently, constitute what could be called a "resistance Nation." Sekou links this nation to the essence of the individual when in the poem he says, "Caribbean manhood / is *cimarron* family is *marronage* nation"; it is not the cruel nation of the Panamanian military leader Noriega or that of the Haitian "ton'ton macoutes," the paramilitary body that served the oppressive dictator François "Papa Doc" Duvalier.

In conversation with him in 2008 and 2010, Sekou presented a brief overview of an aesthetic concept of St. Martin in relation to the slave plantation system, the history of the maroons, and his post-Emancipation theory of the village chief. The following passage is extremely interesting and should be absorbed in its full length to properly appreciate Sekou's suggestion that contemporary politics in the Caribbean was born from a translation of the history of "the unholy slave period":

> During the slave period the plantation system included the enslaved people that worked the fields and mines, the house slaves, and the slave-owning plantocracy. Apart from the plantation during

this period were the maroons ... Pressed to the bottom rung of the plantation by the slave owners there was the brutally exploited enslaved African majority with its hierarchy of "internal" leadership (griots, medicine men and women, culture bearers). The rung cast above the field slaves were the house slaves.... The absolute and oppressive ruling class of the plantation system was the wealthy plantocracy, headed significantly by the European slave masters.... The post-Emancipation or traditional Caribbean societies maintained and even saw reinforced features of the plantation society—especially relative to racial and class hierarchies. George Lamming said that "to truly understand the Caribbean people it is essential to understand the dynamism of Race and Class in the region." Within the post-Slavery political society I point generally to the new ruling elites ..., as replacing but not changing entirely what Edward Said would call "the structures of attitude" (*Culture and Imperialism*) of the plantocracy ... The new house slaves are those who defend uncompromisingly the new elites ... The masses of the people, the working classes ... remain for the most part at the bottom rung of the new dispensation. Fundamental to and at times in the leadership of the ongoing historical transformation of Caribbean societies ... have been: revolutions and revolutionary activities (e.g. Haiti, Cuba, Garveyism, Rastafari as translations of maroon traditions); land reform, labor and independence movements; socio-cultural renaissance and activities (e.g. Negritude, Indigisme, Hosay as a cultural importance to the entire nation of Trinidad and Tobago, carnival); cultural survivals (e.g. foods; medicines; philosophies; dance, song, music and religious forms); deconstruction and reconstruction (e.g. new scholarship perspectives; resiliency, popular and educational uses of Creole languages); political and educational empowerment; and socio-economic developments. These aspects have all in varying degrees and kind been propelling the region beyond the plantation-based structure, its inherited hierarchies, beyond colonial legacies …. In the modern Caribbean it should be made clear too that the activist leadership and support of change for better societies may come from throughout the political society, from throughout the whole social structure, including significantly from the working people.[56]

Sekou's view on Caribbean politics echoes that of the Barbadian writer and thinker George Lamming, who inspired him tremendously. Both embrace the thought of José Martí's, which is expressed in his essay "Our America" ("Nuestra América," 1891), in which Martí criticized the petty view of current political leaders, warning the Latin American "village chiefs" to be wary of the presence and increasing influence of nations that were growing in influence and had great socio-political and economical superpower, and which would ultimately absorb and annul the smaller cultural entities, such as the Caribbean islands. In *Coming, Coming Home*, Lamming makes an interesting observation concerning the role of "village chiefs" in the Caribbean:

> The villager fondly believes that the world is contained in his village and he thinks the universal order good if he can be mayor, humiliate the rival who stole his sweetheart, or add the savings in his sock.... Martí's Village of the nineteenth century has now become a very sophisticated modern design, supervised largely—though not wholly—by an essential village mentality.

A consciousness and self-consciousness of Caribbean manhood, emanating from the region's culture, its complex of cultures, are integral to any improvement of Caribbean society or politics. In his "Nativity," Sekou proclaims that "Culture is marronage." When his work, as in *Quimbé*, takes aim at the link of manhood with the Caribbean "civilization borning," and even in a poem like "preacherman," manhood and nationhood appear as topics and are fortified "at the hands of maroon and genius / and liberation theology / and science and victory / (and love [...])."

This, a type of liberation theology or a doctrine of "foreignism," is suffocated and suppressed by the village chiefs in their repression of the voices of the maroons and of Caribbean people. Here, language and memory enter into the broader relationship and convey Sekou's interpretations of Caribbean manhood and the collective and individual person, relative to historical marronage.

Sekou's *logos*, a word that captures thought and reasoning, is the written reply to oralities that would otherwise be lost in the folds of history. These voices, of maroons and Amerindians, testify to Régis Antoine of the remnants of "ancestral echoes of orality,"[57] defined by him in his article "Paroles perdues de l'Indien et du nègre marron" (1992). The words lost among the historical peoples that mark the struggle for independence are essential notions, symbols, and manifestations of manhood in the aesthetics of a literature. Sekou has published no indication that he would agree with Antoine's discussion of the primordial voice of the maroons as that of a wild and untameable group with a transgressive spirit, counterpoised to the collective voice of the American Indians, as collective, organized groups, cast in a role that Sekou would reject as being nothing more than a newer version of the idea of the noble savage.

Antoine also suggests that the language of neither of the maroons nor of the American Indians is written; thus, both are without *logos*. In *Le discours antillais*, Glissant adds that he considers the maroon to be the real hero of the Caribbean: *"seul vrai héros populaire des Antilles."* However, the tissue that emerges from the weaving of this thread is a *new* voice, teleologically urging an ultimately Caribbean interweaving.

In Sekou's "We Continue," the interweaving of "Gentes de sangre Africana / de sangre Indígena" are "Living through the blood of a world union" in a continuing tradition of resistance, *marronage*, and "fight for liberation," not a remaining echo as described by Antoine, being without *logos*, but instead a "maroonrainstalk," a fighter whose language is imprinted on his or her own skin. On a visit to Barbados, Sekou wrote the poem "bajan," which appears in *The Salt Reaper* and in which he takes note of the "maroonrainstalk" imprinted on the skin of the statue of Bussa, the leader of the island's largest slave uprising, which took place in 1816, and the oozing of pride:

when	pride comes
in	Black
it is	maroonrainstalk
on	Busa colossal skin.

Sekou associates the pride of Caribbean manhood with the symbol of the rooster on at least two occasions. In the poem "Title Deed" from *The Salt Reaper*, "we gaze upon the face of Freedom / and summon her like proud rooster flock / spur off the locks barring the sight from night / from oozing out the maroonspill light of dawn."

In his novella "Brotherhood of the Spurs" the term maroon is used to encompass picnics and cockfights in St. Martin, and the poet readily relates the "he-fowls" who do battle to the maroon spirit of ancient warriors. In this story, the salt pond is also mentioned, and it is associated with the St. Martiners who "once picked salt and rocks to lay the airport runway." In this short work of fiction, the maroon spirit emerges from among the "brothers," the congregation of cockfighting men present, who work together to find a rooster to represent St. Martin that could beat the champion Guadeloupean rooster in a grand upcoming cockfight. For Sekou, the spirit of the maroon warrior emerges from the roosters themselves: Browning, the strongest rooster from St. Martin, is described as a warrior at the start of the short story.

Maroons' call-up

The Akan proverb, "If you allow yourself to forget the sound of your town's horn, you get lost in the gathering" speaks to many features of being, memory, identity, unity, preparedness, call to battle, call to defend, discerning knowledge of self, and ability to negotiate the social, ideational, and active world beyond that of your town. This African saying could be transplanted into Sekou's poetic soil, with its dissemination of calls to freedom and love for the X/Self, to solidarity, to build an independent nation, to fight oppression, and to continue resisting the threat of enslavement and other acts of exploitation, whether they are political, economic, cultural, or historical.

Like the knowledge of the sound of your town's horn, the need for a memory, for hidden heirlooms, and for all the threads of maroon history, is carried by the poet like an Olympic torch across centuries, being fanned by the rhythms of the wind and the sea over which the enslaved people came. It is "The maroon cache of memory manna / i carry," says the poet in *The Salt Reaper's* "yebo." It is through "the coil of our conch-shelled ear," as described in "by the bayside" in *Quimbé,* that we listen to these and other rhythms and catch them. The shell of the conch is a universal symbol of war, victory (maroons), and labor (fisherfolk) throughout the Caribbean region. In Sekou's aesthetics, as in historical *marronage*, the abeng was the iconic instrument that the maroons use to call up and gather the citizens of the maroon camp or nation or to call other maroons to the fight, responding to attacks by soldiers or other armed colonists and authorities of Slavery-based society.

Today's maroons may not blow the actual abeng to warn their fellows against threats and attacks or to organize defenses of themselves and their nations. They may not wear the same clothes as their counterparts during the days of Slavery. To Sekou, the spirit, beliefs, and knowledge-based engagements are merely variations tied to developments and bearing revolutionary links that support his trinity of themes: love, labor, and liberation. In "Taking Form" from *Images in The Yard* (1983), the poet is repeating to a variety of oppressors and to all who will listen, including perhaps some of the oppressed who are listed in the poem, "BEWARE OUR DISGUISE." Perhaps this is a warning against those who believe that the maroon spirit is dead. In "Liberation is Love," in the same collection, Sekou employs expressions from theater and development, crisscrossing, marking, and disguising to imitate the deceitfulness of the politicians who promise food, housing, and clothing to the people while following a different, hidden agenda. The integration of disguise with

> a working consciousness/
> Working hands
> And working minds
>
> Forwarding a new world onward

is also uniquely placed in a new time, in a different setting, in the short story "The Rightful Heirs" from *Love Songs Make You Cry*. Sekou is continually portraying the maroon spirit as adaptable and unconquerable, as still quite alive in the present day, ready to fight current forms of oppression and to *remember*, contributing both symbolically and concretely to the generation of a new aesthetics, to building a new nation, a Caribbean civilization.

Languages of Sekouism

Sekou's knowledge of different languages is evident in his use of them in his writing, from St. Martin English to Caribbean and African languages, to the European languages that mark colonial domination

(English, Dutch, French, Spanish, and German) to Chinese, which bears witness to his time in China as a Visiting Fellow of the International Writers Workshop (IWW) at Hong Kong Baptist University in 2004.

French is to be found in at least three of Sekou's poetry books. In *For The Mighty Gods*, he speaks of love in "Souviendrai": "But we must leave, Ah mon ami, / J'esperai que nous / Recontrerons un jours, / Aurevoir mon amour… / Till another dawn." In the title poem of the *Quimbé* collection, he writes of birth and rebirth, bringing to the reader's attention a natural symbol of the Caribbean, *bois* (wood) "give us new words! to do words of *veuglé, sa çe bois*[58] / children at the window witnessing their own birth / chimes full of laughter: *oui mama!*" French is mixed with Arabic in "the blood boil," the poem on genocide from *The Salt Reaper*: "some are hidden. *se cacher.* […] / *a bon / jour, alaikum salaam.*"

Spanish words are found in the stories and in poems focusing on political issues and questions of immigration. In *Born Here*'s "No Cat," the poet sings, "Be strong, *querida*." In *Quimbé*'s "clarity," too, Spanish appears: "we have been looking at each other / through alien eyes, pale and cruel / *como estranjeros* (...) / clutching at the dante lassos of *el norte* / sat upon *un caballo diablo*," as well as in "immigrants," "But who will soon pay / who will soon run / from *san martin* / from *san materialismo*?"[59]

Following a journey to West Germany in the late 1980s, Sekou wrote "in berlin," published in *Quimbé*. This poem is woven with snippets of German and other languages, like a transformed Dutch, all altered and tied together: "rising specters of *rassismus* / skinhead-bleeding façades of *faschismos*." He summons images of Nazism, fascism, and racism, especially in relation to immigration:

> the afro-look
> of the *schwarzen deutschen*
> and immigrant *menschen* all […]
> and distant *lander* […]
> *wat macht niet* is what you will not)
>
> you are true *sonnen kinder* […]
> this is the *zeitgeist*

and in the following text:

> *luisteren* racist motherfuckers […]
> in *der spiegel* of inwardly brutalized
> races
> this ain' no dibi-dibi "atom-kraft"
> pinned down on its back
> *luisteren allemaal, hort mal alle zu, escuchan pueblo*,
> the victory in unity […].[60]

Sekou's message of "victory in unity," of resistance, and of acceptance of the world beyond the limitations of racism and of the fight against the evils of our world, such as the atomic bomb or acts of violence, is then globalized when he mixes claims in Spanish/Portuguese and German: "*la luta continua / seguro / der kampf geht weiter / tschus*" ["the struggle goes on / for sure / the struggle goes on / bye" NbR].

Badejo further observed that what Brathwaite terms "nation language" is recognized by Sekou under the name "nation tongue."[61] Through his gracious interweaving of languages, Sekou mirrors the multicultural, globalized St. Martiners, while the local peculiarities of St. Martin English,[62] whose grammatical and lexical features he describes in the glossary of *Nativity* and of his short story collections, are also represented.

Sekou engages so deeply with the word that he centers it in his production, from the moment that the word is chosen to the moment of its delivery, whether on the page or in a live reading, and he also creates graphic designs of his poems in his books, arranging the verses and lines to create visual layouts. To indicate pauses for breath in oral delivery, he uses brackets or parentheses; when he needs to accelerate the pace of the reading and to omit pauses he links words, dropping spaces and periods. Fergus observed that "Sekou's 'chirographic' experimentation ... began as early as *Mothernation* and *Quimbé* in 1991."[63] In that latter work, Sekou attacked the barriers between senses, as he equipped every page of the volume with a printed version of the corresponding braille symbol for the number. A blind person would be unable to understand the symbol, flatly printed on the page unable to feel its texture, while most sighted readers would not be able to understand the braille symbol. This apparent paradox shows how Sekou experimented with various techniques and attempted at overcoming disabilities.

In "Nativity," Sekou multiplies word sequences. These repetitions enhance the length of words and the importance they receive from the poet, as early as in "Little Guerrillas" in *For The Mighty Gods*: "I am the front caller-catch up-catch up / Shangoooooooooooooooooooooooooooooooooo." Brathwaite is an inspiration for Sekou's poetry after 1988. The influential Sycorax Video Style (SVS) that Brathwaite developed profoundly marks the "Culture is Self" strophe in "Nativity":

BRAGADANGBAM! Boom si kai si ka boom di la> la la♪♫la♪♫♪♫♪♫♪♫♪♫
♪♫la♪♫la la day>

This is reminiscent of Brathwaite's *bruggalungdum* from "Cane" (1969)[64] or *brugg-a-lung-go* from "The Dust" (1967),[65] which describe the eruption of a volcano.

The poem "r'ass remnants" published in *The Salt Reaper* has as a design on the page a column of acronyms marking territories and definitions, in a rosary of abbreviations targeting imperial politics. The poem, in appearance like a pillar built from colonized territories, puts itself forth like a recitation:

bdt
bot
bvi
bwi
cpr
dc
dwi
fod
fwi
na
upt
dom-tom.&all
like cowbrands
poking usssssssssssssss.still.

In his review of Fergus's *Love Labor Liberation in Lasana Sekou*, Mark Nowak commented that:

> The acronyms identify the remaining colonial territories of the Caribbean region (and the sixteen s's in "us" certainly points to the USAmerican colonial project in the Caribbean (& in Irak, & in Afghanistan, & in...).[66]

Fergus observed that:

> The acronyms—identifying the remaining colonial territories in the Caribbean region—work visually, they goad (poke) us like asses while branding us with an external identity.[67]

The recitation of the whole poem on the CD of *The Salt Reaper* sounds like a composition in rap, with the final "still," needed to keep up the pace of the poem, and the final prolonged "us" becomes similar to the sound of applying a branding iron to cattle skin. In his reading, Sekou pronounces "dom-tom" as "dumb tom."[68]

This graphic appearance, and the division of a poem into columns resurfaces in "title." This verse from *37 Poems* appears to be split into two columns, divided by the delivery of different, or ciphered, messages:

title   X

militants&insurgents
come to be
                           +males of military age+
new code for the coders
a codeX.a con-
stitute to "hunt them down"
                           +marked man+
come to be
all who look so all alike
my brothers, again, the dark mane
locks in the cross hairs.   +

Here, Sekou is not employing Dread Talk,[69] but a first reading appears to indicate that Rastafarian militancy is being discussed. In communication following my first interview with Sekou, this short poem grew in interest for me due to its simplicity combined with a density of symbols. For the poet, there is a comparative identification between the "militants&insurgents" of contemporary war who "look so all alike" and Black men in the Caribbean, the Americas, and Europe, as arises from the interpretation of the two sequential lines containing the words "my brothers," "dark mane," and "locks in the cross hairs." The word "brothers" and the Afro hair, appearing as a "dark mane," could symbolize the Black Panthers, echoing the racist in the US who would say that "all Blacks look alike," a perspective that was not unfamiliar in literature. The lion's mane and the locks of hair relate to the dark mane symbols of Rastafari, which identified Rastafarians for persecution by the police and subjected them to much discrimination, both official and unofficial, throughout the Caribbean between from the 1950s to the 1980s. "My brothers, again" and "locks in the cross hairs" bring up current news images of young, very often poor Black and Latino men ("+males of military age+"), who are so often targets of street shooting or other forms of abuse, around the world.

The extension of Sekou's concerns in space and time reveals his extensive, encyclopedic knowledge. During his stay in Hong Kong and Beijing, he developed his series of "Hong Kong poems," which appear in *37 Poems*.[70] In the former English colony of Hong Kong, which returned to Chinese control in 1997, Sekou is aware of the city's multiculturalism, such as its foreign domestic workers in their gatherings on the weekends[71] or appearing in the encounter among Western and Eastern cultures, languages, and religions, expressing relationships with the Other in postcolonial terms, as the poet describes it in this section of a slim volume, "the other *feng shui*." In fact, the Filipinas (a reference to the Filipino maids who arrive in Hong Kong for work mostly from the Philippines, a former Spanish colony) are shown attending the Christian mass in the poem "hong kong sunday." Again, Sekou visually renders what he writes, playing with alliteration and layouts, as "in Central.ground like crop circles." Here, in a Christian church, echoing with Spanish prayers, *"aquí.avemarías y más.niñas,"* a central building appears, in a pagan architecture, following the principles of Chinese geomancy or *"feng shui"* and resounding with tones of the Chinese violin, the *"erhu,"* in "weep to wail to worry to win."

Another string instrument that appears or is alluded to in this collection is the ancient *qin* or *gu zheng*, in the poem "xinXin." The peculiar title of this piece could be read as a transliteration of either of the Mandarin words 新 *(xīn)* = new or 心 *(xīn)* = heart. The first tonal reading seems to fit the underlying theme of love that is peculiar to this poem, as "heart-heart" or "a new heart." Nonetheless, the Mandarin *xīn* is quite close in sound to the word 星 *(xīng)* = star, leaving perhaps a hint at the stars on the flag of the People's Republic of China, which form a crescent, a "crest-sacred / iron." Sekou likely saw the Forbidden City, the imperial palace in the center of Beijing, which could lead to a bird's-eye view perspective on the events that have made up China's history, like the Japanese invasion of Nanking (Nanjing) in 1937, the "nanjing mass- / acre" and the "nankin mask," or Tiananmen Square, "twice branded rouge." *Quimbé's* "in berlin" had already invoked Tiananmen in connection with an international cluster of mostly young demonstrators:

> chasing ton-ton macouts from the streets of haiti
> forcing wide open democracy's boulevards
> in chile … in the kwangju of korea
> peopling the tiananmen square of china

Furthermore, in "xinXin," Sekou refers to the Chinese political activist and poet Beidao (born Zhang Zhenkai). This "mad poet" is a catalyst for the territory, suitably enough for his name 北岛 (běi dǎo), which means "northern island," an emotional territory where Sekou could mirror and mystify his own: "still no misty beidao in sight / i see no mad poets wording for cold miners."

In "xinXin," we experience more than wordplay and literary allusions to the political importance of poets and their identification with the land, on the opposite side of the world from St. Martin, but also to the reality that the world is small and in Antonio

Benítez-Rojo's words is constituted of "repeating islands." Wordplay interweaves with alliteration, and the page is a smithy of creativity and revelation of Sekou's own life and of language. The color red here becomes first *roseau* and then *rouge*, while the words "ghosts, guests, and just" mingle together. Sounds and letters join the game in "let the beijing bus ride pass by / and miss bai and i, the growl of a breakfastless rush." In Sekou's understanding of the politics of the world and its philosophy, he is exploring by reduction whether Communism can be viable in practical terms: "talk and mao on the money and marx on lit / theory and in practice." Sekou then depicts himself discussing history with Miss Bai, a university student assigned to the group as guide,[72] who may be the owner of the pair of eyes that made him forsake the Forbidden City:[73] "i forsook the forbidden city / for a perfect set of eyes"; is this why, in his introduction to *37 Poems*, the Indian literary critic Tabish Khair said that in this poem "Love is also combined with larger concerns"?[74]

In another poem, Sekou records a visit to the island of Lantau in Hong Kong by Cynthia James, author of *The Maroon Narrative, Caribbean Literature in English Across Boundaries, Ethnicities and Centuries* (2002). On the top of a hill on this "worker island" stands "the Buddha brilliant regime in sun," a titanic bronze statue that represents the enlightened. At Buddhist temples it is common "to shake sticks at the… future," a religious practice called 求签 *(qiúqiān)*, in which a cylinder that is full of numbered sticks is agitated, and from which a stick falls that corresponds to a numbered piece of paper that contains a prediction of the future of the petitioner. James, also an IWW Visiting Fellow, is shown visiting the shacks of the poor in fishing villages, far from the most commonly visited tourist destinations.

The poet explores on his own as well. Hong Kong's Wang Jiao district and Nathan Road are mentioned in the poem "father guide": "mongkok at night / […] / along nathan road" and "kowloon tong." The setting seems to be the time of preparation for the Chinese Lunar New Year, which falls in January or February, as is suggested by the lines "in the wake of the dragon's full claim" and "like longing for these tall eve days to christmas / and look on to the new year's coming of this world". In "going home," which describes the end of the narrated journey, on a plane back to his native "I-land," Sekou sounds nostalgic:

> over the east china sea
> caressing up and along the dragon breast of japan
> the iron beast stretches, wings it.

During Sekou's time as a literary fellow in Hong Kong, he also recorded some of his work for his first audio CD, *The Salt Reaper—selected poems from the flats* (2009). This collection does not fail to travel all around the world, bringing together salsa, bachata, jazz, kalimba, electronic music, steel pan, Spanish guitar, African drums,[75] and, of course, the power of the poet's voice. The music, mixed by the St. Martin digital artist Angelo Rombley, enhances the quality of the oral delivery, so that the performance is enlightening, refreshing, and qualitatively strong. Sometimes thanks to Rombley's eclectic selection of beats and at other times thanks to his own rhythmic repetitions of words, Sekou sounds like a dub poet. Some of the poems selected are local; some are regional, like "El Malecòn" ("The Waterfront," describing the Dominican Republic), where a Spanish guitar echoes the colonial roots of the island; and some are more global, touching on the sociopolitical problems that threaten Black communities around the world or others that are common to people everywhere.

The *Salt Reaper* CD appears to be a natural product of Sekou's experimentation with oral and scribal expression and music *riddims*. This poetic and musical production brought him new audiences in St. Martin, where it was played on the radio and described by the kaiso historian Fernando Clark as "Relentless music, contemporary ... classical tones" that "amplify the lyrical content of Lasana's work."[76] The sounds of *The Salt Reaper* are heard off the island as well. "Poems accompanied by hurtling hot music" was "A brilliant move!" as Amiri Baraka, the revolutionary US poet and quintessential blues/jazz historian, commented.[77]

Since 1978, Sekou has been praising musicians and singers and putting their musical messages forward in his works. In *Moods for Isis*, we can find the poem "Rasta Song" alongside a drawing of a Rastafarian. He also evokes the Trinidadian calypso or kaiso in "Tribute": "Hail the MIGHTY DUKE / The rebel lord of *caiso* [...] / We must "Teach the Children" / "Black is Back"[...] / Go on mighty composer / Chant your tropical rhymes / And stir the sleeping minds." Ten years later, in "Nativity," Sekou continued to show his attraction to the indigenous musical genres of Trinidad and Tobago, as well as to its variations and the singers from St. Martin and around the Caribbean. In "Nativity," the long poem from 1988, he renders calypso or kaiso as an undulating, musical rhythm, without pauses between the words, singing "Weiskaisoborninthecanefields." This line, describing cultural or historical consciousness, leads into verses by the St. Martin calypsonian Mighty Dow speaking of the joy of singing and making music: "shantybongocalypsoooooooooooooooooooooooooo / and we sing / and we sing / and we sing again." Here, the vowel "o" is extended to express a shout or intonation. Sekou takes care to express as much as possible with his words, such that although the words lie flat on the page, they are nevertheless heard by the reader, as well as being seen, as in the visual reproductions of eighth and sixteenth in his line, as a way of paying tribute to the seminal importance of music:

> la> la la♪♫la♪♫♪♫♪♫♪♫♪♫♪♫
> ♪♫la♪♫la la day>

The repetition of sounds may even begin to sound like a children's rigmarole:

> Culture jam sessions
> with a pingpingpingalinglingpanupponpan
> Spreeofsteeldrums.

This characteristic is present in both editions of this work. Christopher Winks reviewed *Nativity / Nativité / Natividad—Trilingual Edition* in the *Caribbean Vistas Journal* (2014) and called it "Epic in scope."[78] Here, how Sekou expands his concept of a musical Caribbean aesthetics is essential, expressing himself through the steel pan, which allows a seamless weaving in and out of other music genres and of historical pain, geopolitical protest, language play, and mystical space. Thus,

> if you think you lost the pangs
> and panalanglangsteelarkestras
> arkestrating pan vibes
> > pan Caribbean
> > pan *Caribe*
> > pan *Antilles*
> > pan people are nation (pan)
> > the world pan
> > against apartheid
> > andpanapanfree
> pan you, pan eye, pan *oui*
> fire-laced oilpots of steel cooktune

In her introduction to the first edition of *Nativity*, Gumbs noted that "The 'pan' themes are…synthesized in a revolutionary cultural holism that materializes, and when it feels like, mythologizes…."

Apart from kaiso and pan, Sekou embeds other types of music and song indigenous to the Caribbean and the Americas in his poetry. In the "Culture winds. winds us culturewise" section of "Nativity," he sequences the symbol for "wise," from the distinguished intellectual tradition of C.L.R.

James to the ultimate music rebel, Bob Marley, to contemporary inventive dub, including references to the reggae of The Wailers, all driving the shanty, a work sea-song, which dissolves in a wordplay in the wail of a "whalesong":

> C.L.R.wise, Bobwise, dubwise.
> Make us
> wail like wailers wailing whalesong

The intention of this work could be to communicate how culture moves us and "Make[s] us wail," both through consciousness and in a mysterious way. In this reading of Sekou's aesthetics, it may be best to appreciate how sweet and soulful those undulating lines are that offer to carry us away, "wailing," to other marvelous interpretations of mind, music, dance, and song.

In *Quimbé*, Sekou defines *quimbé* as the "topical St. Martin song, sung in a fast-paced singsong without musical accompaniment. [Composed and sung up to the mid-20 c.; orig. unkn.]." The title poem of this collection mixes the pace of *quimbé* with jazz rhythms á la Brathwaite, alluding to or quoting a conscious hip-hop group: "rap link / x-clangangstarbustingraysfull: it's like a jazz thing." In Sekou's fusion of genres, the poet blends not only music and song but other cultural forms as well to deepen or intensify aspects of the poem, its message, and the aesthetics that it expresses. For instance, art is interfused in the poem "quimbé," with its reference to Roland Richardson, a leading Caribbean impressionist painter, who immortalized the St. Martin "national tree," the flamboyant. Sekou draws a connection among this tree, the people's celebration of Emancipation, and folk tales:

> give us paint flamboyant fierce
> give us lasting songs of treacherously defiant lyrics
> like roland's battery of flora
> surging sorties off canvas ablaze against gloom sky
> blasted blazing blooming

Sekou incorporates aspects of St. Martin's *ponum* dance, with its African origins, dominant drumming, and the accompanying "Brim song" in his poetic fusion.[79] The glossary for *Nativity* describes the *ponum* as a "traditional dance, has origin in fertility rites and harvest celebrations, reportedly danced on St. Martin's Emancipation Day" in 1848.

The poem "cradle of the nation" from *The Salt Reaper* expresses the genre fusion among multiple types of art in varied ways. In one instance, the dance and music of St. Martin are illustrating what appears to be, within the bloody remains of the work of

Slavery, a courtship ritual in the waters of the Great Salt Pond:

> your steps stout to a quimbé
> trace through the canyons of brine, courted her a home.
> you&she.Divine in ponum (...)

In *Born Here*, Sekou begins to write in a way that conforms to his own notion of aesthetics. "On Caribbean Aesthetics," appearing in that volume, which is his first poem to include the word aesthetics, the poet clearly shows himself on the road to his own form. Music and dance, as name and symbol, are within in the mix, and he admits:

> I still question
> The way my fathers danced
> While our mothers bore children
> Stooped in labor over the clean Salt Ponds of Great Bay
> Where you can still see them
> Chanting ponums
> For the hills and people to mirror themselves
> In mornings of reflection
> When the water turns to still sheets of glass

In the ensuing decade, Sekou characterizes the Great Salt Pond in this way: "The man-made pollution of the great pond, from the dump heap, septic run-off, and encroaching landfill, is such that the 'still sheets of glass' feature for the St. Martin 'people to mirror themselves' is practically no more." In response, he crafts the 1996 poem "Great Salt Pond Speaks," a lament that is fused with symbols of dance and music, both folk and contemporary: "Ponum! Ponum! I am belching back a stench. You stifle your / nose holes, cry" and "*A-Buyaka! Buyaka! Becausin I am a bomb of poison.* [...] / *Buyaka. and retaliate, Salt Pond! Re-ta-li-aaaaaaaaaaaaaaaaaaaaate!*" The *buyaka* (heard in dancehall songs; and as "booyaka" in the 1992 kaiso "Dus' in Dey Face" by David Rudder) is an invocation to retaliate, to fight back.

Sekou's poetry includes music and dance more so in essence, as a symbol, or for their rhythms. Here, he finds common ground with Rombley, who has been responsible for translating some of Sekou's poems into short films, in which the visual effects, the power of words, and the musical accompaniment all serve to convey the poet's central message of political contests, criticism of the abuses of society, social injustice, and the crimes of history.

The film *casualtiesFX3* (2009) was created around the poem "casualties," found on the CD *The Salt Reaper*. Sekou embraces the cause of war victims and prisoners of war from around the world, reviewing the horrors of the day committed upon people by the systems that should be protecting them from becoming casualties. This work opens the door to the image that "torture is a/nakedheap," accompanied by a picture of the Haitian Abner Louima, arrested and abused by New York City police. Then a transition is made to Abu Ghraib in Baghdad and the abuses of the US–Iraq war; to Mazar-e-Sharif in Afghanistan; and to the Guantanamo Bay detention camp, in a part of Cuba that is occupied by the US. The mixture of music and images produced by Rombley also exhibit aeroplanes spreading needless death among victims of war. This poem concludes in part by goading the reader on to care, to correct, and to prevent these and other atrocities, bearing battered, almost crippled, and crucified images of hope:

> in war
> love is still well. tattered battered shattered awake
> justice never tires the knobkneed hunchbacked
> googlieeyed assent to grace
> peace is a/brew /a bitters cup to take.

As audio plays of the poet's recitation, Rombley portrays images of people in the fields, unaware of the planes overhead as those target them and release their bombs to make the people casualties of war, spilling their blood as water in their fields.

This video underlines Sekou's role as, in Fergus's characterization, "a poet of war."[80]

Another of Rombley's production *Final roughneck* (2009), a provocative 1:06-minute video to accompany the poem "Roughneck," collected in *The Salt Reaper* recordings. Here words crisscross and encounter each other on the screen, superimposing one on the other, together with an aggressive recital by the poet of these lines:

> There is a poem coming
> it is
> & not
> for recital
> refined & respectful
> this poem has no regard
> for women & children
> & some should do well to be distant from it now

Sekou's words here take aim at the reader of the poem, the viewer, the audience, pushing toward action, to stir each one inside with the tough and direct choice of words and the passionate performance. Sekou's final message in this film is an exhortation to fight and resistance:

> succession time come to say
> Caribbean man
> S'maatin man

study to do
step up for your land, unbound the captive nation
with reason&rightness.

The use of various colors in the videos, as in the stark red shown in *casualtiesFX3* and in the presentation of words in others, bears meaning as well. *Final roughneck* is an illustrative example of the fruitful combination of color, image, and text. At the beginning of this film, the word roughneck appears in white on a black screen. Then more words appear, and their appearance accelerate, as they are being recited by Sekou, appearing now in white and now in red, popping out onto the screen, one after the other. In place of showing the bowls of the letters as small holes, they instead appear as crosses and small x shapes, recalling the letter that is very present in the poem "title x." As this poem progresses, the words take on new colors and seem to crowd the screen in a confusion of hues. However, it is only toward the end of the video that the words "man," "studytodo," and "nation" are shown in the Rastafarian colors, red, yellow, and green, indicating the righteous message that Caribbean people must study to create a nation.

Sekou's solo and choral voice

Sekou's poetic voice forms part of a Caribbean counterpoint. His commitment to the cause of his people and to humanity in general is thrown into relief in his approach to historical, political, and economic causes; local, regional, and international social challenges; and his own aesthetics, which is rooted in his linguistic choices: the construction of a creole voice and a maroon voice. Fergus, Badejo, Rodríguez, and Nowak recognize Sekou's innovativeness, and the importance of history, politics, and language to his aesthetics.[81] In the extension of Sekou's voice to a choral one, his work expresses a Caribbean aesthetics. Dr. Conrad M. James hailed *Nativity / Nativité / Natividad* as a "triumph of Caribbean aesthetics."[82]

Sekou's "On Caribbean Aesthetics," from *Born Here*, appears particularly pregnant in this connection. In that poem Sekou strives to stir the conscience of his people: "Don't just sit there, now / Get up! / Ask the fucking CBI (Caribbean Bourgoise Intellectuals) / What they mean / That our Caribbean aint got no aesthetics?" This poem touches on all the themes we have found in Sekou's work: the theme of salt, the importance of spirituality and its African elements and symbols, the maroons, and Sekou's commitment to the political improvement of St. Martin. In the poem an encounter with a "priestess" is described. Sekou's St. Martin forebears are mentioned in connection to their hard labor in the Great Salt Pond, which helped build St. Martin into what it is nowadays, with the pond playing the role of a mirror for society and for the history of the land. The priestess invites the poet to drink sweat, perhaps drawing the poet closer to a reunion with his ancestors, to bond with them and create a link with them, enhancing the spiritual meaningfulness of the rite beyond the place where the poet, at the threshold of the poem, can say:

> I have watched my fathers
> Dancing in the shadow of iguanas
> Skanking in the light of goatskin drums
> In the arch of Legba's limbo
> Where I still question their songs
> Sealed in the foot prints of their absence (...)

Sekou is a living example of what the poet John La Rose asserted to be the meaning of poetry in *Eyelets of Truth Within Me* (1992). To La Rose, poets absorb and pass on the past to understand our mistakes as human beings and produce love and hope to create a better society:

We are ... the living tissue of contemporaneity caught in islands, or thicker land masses, plying our own triangular trade in ourselves, exporting ourselves from hopelessness into hope ... and lived to fight. ... We are the salted embryo of a world whose fixities grow loose.

EVOLUTION OF A "WEST INDIAN" AESTHETICS

> *I have studied history
> in the thick buttresses of
> their roots.*
>
> – Earl McKenzie
>   "The Old Cotton Trees Are Dying"

Aesthetic flourishes and solos in a Caribbean poetic ensemble

Examination of the evolutionary development of Caribbean literature would discover a vivid literary panoply that, it could be argued, was first opened as such by Louis Morpeau. In his article on the muse of Haitian creole, published in Paris in the *Anthologie d'un Siècle de Poésie Haïtienne 1817–1925* (1925), he stressed the importance of orality:

> This linguistic mosaic, in constant evolution towards more harmony, clarity, purity and finesse in the purely phonetic orthography and in pronunciation, will give birth to an extremely picturesque, vivid, literature, full of imagery, but above all an oral literature.[83]

A deeper overview of the existence of a "West Indian" aesthetics would begin in the late 1940s and extend to the early 1950s, when writers and authors like Saint-John Perse, Shake Keane, Martin Carter, and Derek Walcott began to express their own views. In his 1952 article "Some Religious Attitudes in W.I. Poetry. The Orthodox Attitude and Variations," the Vincentian poet Keane recognizes a true budding of literature in the late 1940s and speaks of "W.I. Literary Bourgeonnement,"[84] which came to attention in terms of its "strict metre and rigid rhyme-scheme."[85]

The Windrush generation that moved to the UK in the 1950s (including Sam Selvon, George Lamming, and Wilson Harris) influenced the canons of West Indian aesthetics, because those writers, native to the once- (or still-) colonized Caribbean islands were confronting those previously dominating cultures, which had such a profound impact on how they wrote literature. Something needed to be broken, and the zest of the peculiar nature of Caribbeaness required unleashing by the subsequent independence movements, like the Jewel movement in 1970s Grenada and the unrest that came to Guyana.

Walcott bitterly argues in his 1957 article "Society and the Artist" that "There is no serious West Indian artist, painter or poet, who would not prefer to say something of his country rather than give a view of Venice. Europe does not belong to them."[86] This proclamation of non-belonging underlined the fact that literature, and poetry in particular, was scarcely read or published in the Caribbean, leaving aside the possibility that it could support a writer.

However, Guadeloupe-born Saint-John Perse's definition of the nature of poetic aesthetics reached its deepest clarity when the language of science was brought to bear, binding the quintessence of art and expression:

> by virtue also of a language through which is transmitted the supreme rhythm of Being, the poet clothes himself in a transcendental reality to which the scientist cannot aspire. ... Poetry is not only a way of knowledge; it is even more a way of life—of life in its totality.[87]

This remark, which forms part of his acceptance speech for the 1960 Nobel Prize in Literature, is underpinned by a deep sense of history,[88] exhibiting a certain spirituality, expressing a sense that poetry is imbued with the divine essence of God, raising its aesthetic rhythms further above the achievements of science. Perse's meditations on transcendence are linked with his thoughts on immanence because in his conception, the beauty of poetry is both transcendent and immanent, stemming from the revelatory nature of its expression from the core of things.

Acknowledging that literature embodies power and the ability to express the inner beauty of things, Caribbean literature was forced to find its own shape, self-grown expressing its own contours and peculiarities. In a word, it had to go native, bear its own local flavor, renounce its Europeanness. It had to embrace what O.R. Dathorne called in *Caribbean Verse, An Anthology* (1967) a "West Indianization of the English Literature and Language." In *Poems and Stories of St. Christopher, Nevis and Anguilla* (1960), edited by the Kittitian John Brown, this process was expressed. In Brown's foreword to his anthology, he showed that for a West Indian literary aesthetics to be defined, a West Indian identity was needed as well:

> I would suggest ... that the most successful of West Indian writers are, and are likely to be, those whose ears are most sensitively attuned to the characteristic rhythms of speech of their people, to their characteristic ways of expression and thus to their essential ways of thought and feeling. It is, too, particularly necessary at this time of the West Indian search for identity, a search to define their own social, cultural and racial values, that their roots should not be turned away from.

Brown recognized the need to express the unifying features of the whole archipelago, to give a higher and more extended concept of unity, also respecting the fact that the writers were intending to reproduce local features of language in their work, the speech, rhythm, and intonation of the Caribbean, as landmarks that shape the identity of aesthetics in the region. Needless to say, the issue of identity is seen to be among the most important in postcolonial scholarly writing, as well as being a strong need in our globalized society. Today, identities are hybrid, multi-faceted, and polyglot, and the boundaries of belonging are being entirely reshuffled and reconfigured in the moment that this is being written. Our identarian conscience is also shifting the way it self-reflects.

Brown's collection of poems and folk stories naturally brings the best-known Jamaican storyteller to mind, Louise Bennett, a member of the Order of Merit of Jamaica and an honorary Doctor of Letters from York University of Toronto. Through her life and work, Bennett enhanced the importance of orality and oral devices in creole poetry, contributing in a way that was similar to how the Jamaican writer Claude McKay did after his discovery by the English ethnologist Walter Jekyll, who encouraged his work. Dathorne, in his anthological work, foregrounded folk traditions in Caribbean literature, unifying the scribal and visual–aural dimensions of it, saying,

> Equally no direct link can be said to exist between modern West Indian poets and folk-songs … The dialect verse of Claude McKay and Louise Bennett could not have been written without this folk-tradition which is to do with a new way of seeing as well as of hearing.

Even though Dathorne's conception of the "West Indianization of the English Literature and Language," found in a dive into folk traditions and orality, the related poetry remained subject to criticism. The genre was considered of low quality, as expressed in John Figueroa's observation in *Dreams and Visions*, the first volume he edited of *Caribbean Voices: An Anthology of West Indian Poetry* (1966): "I belonged to a people without a literature. … It was not great poetry." Although this may appear to be an unfairly negative idea of a growing literature, West Indian literature at first was centered around the novel, a form of writing that Walcott recognized as largely poetic.[89] The importance of folk traditions for the definition of identity gained prominence in the Caribbean Artists Movement (CAM). One of the foremost voices in this group, that of the Trinidadian poet and critic Marina Ama Omowale Maxwell, who was living in London in the mid-1960s, declared that this underpinning had primary importance in the definition of a Caribbean aesthetics, as she stated in her collection of essays *About Our Own Business* (1981). Omowale Maxwell was recognized by Kamau Brathwaite as a revolutionary in his essay "CR, the Caribbean Revolution in the arts."

Up until the 1970s, the peculiarity of using West Indian tones in literature, which extended the possibilities of the English language, was recognized by Figueroa. In *Caribbean Voices: An Anthology of West Indian Poetry, Volume 1*, he stated that, "the West Indian poet is already contributing to the growth and texture of the English language by the use he makes of it, when writing in his own voice and with his special Caribbean structures and rhythms." In the second volume of this anthology, entitled *The Blue Horizons*, Figueroa foregrounded the linguistic aspects of West Indian literature. He also defined the figure of the West Indian writer and, following the Guyanese writer Slade Hopkinson, "West Indianismus."[90] His analysis extended the umbrella and the limits or extension of the West Indian continuum and West Indian Standard English.

In 1960, the above-mentioned Saint-John Perse was awarded the Nobel Prize in Literature, and the

St. Lucian Sir Arthur Lewis received the Nobel Memorial Prize for Economy in 1979. Lewis's 1971 essay "On Being Different" is particularly poignant from an aesthetic point of view, as in it he compares West Indian thought relative to its possible contribution to "human heritage," asserting that

> It is thus of the very nature of the game that as aesthetic activity burgeons in the West Indies, our art and music and literature will be clearly distinguishable from that of other peoples. We shall have our own schools of painting and music and poetry and drama and the rest. This is the essential and most valuable sense in which West Indians must be different from other peoples. This is the contribution which above all others we know we can make to the common human heritage.[91]

Of particular notice in the 1970s discussion and development of a West Indian aesthetics was the so-called Savacou debate, which took place among West Indian and non-West Indian writers and scholars. It was named after *Savacou* ¾ (1970), an anthology that Brathwaite edited. The writers' responses to the appearance of this volume had many aspects. The debate largely revolved around the importance of orality to Caribbean literature and the legitimacy of the employment of creole, shifting from the nature of musicality in poetry to the interpenetration of the oral and scribal modes of writing. The Tobagonian Eric Roach dismissed the anthology. However, the Guyanese scholar Gordon Rohlehr and Trinidadian poets such as Roger McTair and Syl Lowhar criticized Roach's attack. After Roach's suicide in 1974, the Trinidadian poet Wayne Brown wrote a poem that condemned all those "carrion" who had led Roach to suicide, to which Rohlehr replied in his essay "A Carrion Time."[92]

The "Savacou debate" was fundamentally a cumbersome exchange among writers and scholars, but it tackled one of the most important points in Caribbean literature, that is, the relevance of orality and of the employment of creoles in literature. In those years, the 1960s and 1970s, the issues of Blackness and "Africanity" had gained prominence in large part due to the Black Power Movement in the US and the UK, mirrored by the re-emergence of the image and ideas of Marcus Garvey. Likely the issues of the period in which the discussion took place prompted Brown's view that the debate was promoting ideas of Africanness, following the Black Power Movement.[93]

As the Savacou discussion heated up, the poetry anthology *La poésie antillaise* (1977), edited by the Guadeloupean writer Maryse Condé, was published in Paris. In her introduction, Condé indicated the relevance of poetry to defining Caribbean socio-aesthetics, in the fact that poetry and society walk hand in hand.[94] In this she was inspired by Suzanne Césaire's 1941 definition of "French Caribbean" literature, as a sweetened, exoticized version for tourists:

> Suzanne Césaire écrit à leur sujet dans la revue *Tropiques* qui naîtra des années plus tard en 1941: « Littérature de hamac. Littérature de sucre et de vanille. Tourisme littéraire...Allons, la vraie poésie est ailleurs. Loin des rimes, des complaintes, des alizés, des perroquets. Bambous, nous décrétons la mort à la littérature doudou. Et zut à l'hybiscus, à la frangipane, aux bougainvilliers. » [95]

In a Caribbean socio-aesthetics, derivative and stereotypical exoticism should be avoided, a perspective that in *Coming, Coming Home*, Lamming traced to "the status of exotic and eccentric report to that of text as a genuine, organic report, of experience of a specific social reality (in other words, the inventory of an identifiable fold)."

If it is imperative to set literature free from cultural, political, and economic dependence, the key to bringing forth what Condé called "Antillanité," then Glissant was the most prominent personality of the Francophone Caribbean,[96] producing the massive theoretical work *Le discours antillais* (1981), in which he created a theory of Caribbean aesthetics, history, society, and civilization. Glissant brought forth a socio-aesthetics from the observation of Caribbean camouflage, the set of disguising stratagems under which Caribbean history concealed itself underground, in the Brathwaitian sense of "submarine unity," making that nourishing, vital sap and linking the whole chain of Caribbean islands and territories underwater, as he expressed in the journal *Savacou*.[97] Michael Dash's translation of *Le discours antillais* as *Caribbean Discourse: Selected Essays* (1989) revealed Glissant's deconstructionist and metamorphic nature as a writer and theoretician,[98] also bringing to the fore his wide aesthetic imagination, extending from his historical analysis of the region and its literature:

> In this tangle of new forms, this verbal carnality, Glissant visualizes the poetics of *Antillanité*. This idea stands in clear opposition to the longing for the virtues of clarity and the disincarnate aesthetic of those who wished to suppress the cross-cultural imagination.

Through this consistent metaphor, Glissant becomes, in Dash's words, an Orpheus-like poet, with "The capacity of the writer descend, like Orpheus, into the underworld of the collective unconscious and to emerge with a song that can reanimate the petrified world."

The figure of Orpheus and his subterranean myth seem to fit Brathwaite's conception of Caribbean unity as submarine, along with the idea that Caribbean poets play a federating role, enabled by their use of creole and *nation language*.[99] Because orality and scribality appear to coexist and cohabitate in the poetry of the region, reception has played a role in this process of fusion. A relative reading of Benitez-Rojo's *The Repeating Island*, posits that a written text, as pre-text, can become a text only if it is engaged in a binomial relationship with the reader, who will absorb and share or reject the text. Artistic productivity in the Caribbean is related to the identity of the people and their resistance in artistic or performative scenes. Their resonance produces an echo from one island to another, as each island of the Caribbean archipelago forms part of a post-plantation system, repeating a texture and a fragmented historiographic pattern made of uprootedness and re-routedness.

Glissant pushes this analogy further in *Le discours antillais*, comparing the work of Brathwaite with that of other poets working in different parts of the Caribbean, such as Léon-Gontran Damas, from

Cayenne in French Guiana on the north coast of South America, or the Cuban poet Nicolàs Guillén. The native languages of these three poets are English, French, and Spanish, but Glissant prompts agreement with his statement that all three draw from history and similarly employ orality in their poetry, "L'écrit s'oralise." Glissant sets Brathwaite's and Walcott's poetics alongside each other. The former conceives the literature of the Caribbean as an underwater history, while the latter identifies history with the sea: "Et Derek Walcott, dans son tout dernier recueil de poèmes: «History is Sea»."

Again, the notion of history and of Caribbean *riddim* in *nation language* was a benchmark conclusion in Brathwaite's 1977 essay "Love Axe: Developing a Caribbean Aesthetic" and of his 1979 lecture at Harvard University, published in 1984 as *History of the Voice*, in which Brathwaite underlined Glissant's definition of *nation language*:

> the language of enslaved persons. For him, nation language is a strategy: the slave is forced to use a certain kind of language in order to disguise himself, to disguise his personality and to retain his culture. And he defines that language as "forced poetics" because it is a kind of prison language.[100]

A different definition of the role of the artist in the Caribbean artist, found in a developed socio-aesthetic context, was discussed in 1979 both by Martin Carter and Gordon Rohlehr. In his essay "The Location of the Artist," Carter acknowledged the lack of satisfaction and fulfillment that is linked to self-consciousness as a reason to justify negative productivity in the artist in Guyana and the correspondent displacement.[101] In his essay "Articulating a Caribbean Aesthetic: The Revolution of Self-Perception," Rohlehr wrote that the process of marronage, which began from within slaves as resistance, was the real artistic revolution:

> The "revolution of self-perception" really began with the inner resistance of the slaves to the self, imposed on them by the plantation system and slavery. In its most fundamental form it was the refusal to be a thing, an object, a tool, mere chattel: the *negation of a process of reification*. The positive aspect of this revolution involved *the constant affirmation of the validity of the submerged self*, the self—to borrow Edward Kamau Brathwaite's phrase—in maroonage; the marooned, submerged and often subversive self. This *self-in-maroonage* was affirmed in infinite ways.[102]

Funso Aiyejina characterized the Caribbean artist in his 1987 article "Derek Walcott: The Poet as a Federated Consciousness" as having a federating role.[103] This is a role of reconstruction, as Badejo put it in his introduction to Brathwaite's *Words Need Love Too* (2000). This federative role concerns the incorporation of history and of traditions, as well as of music, orality, and wordplays. This syncretic conception of poetry is quite present in Sekou, who incorporates the ancestral music of his home island into his "performance poetry."[104] In *Salted Tongues*, Badejo lets out some intriguing remarks on St. Martin literature and Caribbean aesthetics, linking the author to the text and to its reception, both by society and by critics:

> The dialectic interplay between the text, the author, the society, and the critic must be one that unveils the inherent contradictions in our existential reality and point to possible solutions. Similarly, the criteria the critic uses in the analysis of the text must reflect a distinctively Caribbean aesthetics.[105]

Thus, literary criticism should uncover the essence of aesthetics, which, in the case of the remaining Netherlands territories in the Caribbean, is united by a common historical background, although it is also different from the nature of other islands, as the insularity of each is contested by the cultural melting pot of cultures that do not appear in other parts of the Caribbean: in St. Martin (both parts), for instance, people from many and various parts of the world are living together.

This variety is enhanced by today's tendency toward globalization, which is developing a higher sense of belonging and a constant redefinition of frontiers and cultural borders in this twenty first-century globalized world. Rex Nettleford puts a similar claim forward in "The Caribbean's Creative Diversity: the Defining Point of the region's History," a lecture given in Guyana in 2003:

> The entire world is gone "creole"—in the Caribbean sense of forging from the disparate elements of a "village-world" new expressions challenging us all to a new ontology, a new cosmology and, by extension, a new epistemology.[106]

Nettleford observes the cultural production of the nations of the Caribbean region from a bird's-eye view and searches for unity in epistemological terms, although he also recognized that "The products may differ one from another but the region shares a similar process of becoming." Many cultural personalities of the Caribbean recognize a similar unification in difference: C.L.R. James, in 1961, found in it a

> strange, a unique combination of the greatest driving force in the world today, the underdeveloped

formerly colonial colored peoples ... [who] began [their] historical existence in a highly developed modern society—the sugar plantation.

These words are recalled in Sekou's 2007 lecture "Color & Cultural Identity: A Caribbean Story," in which he declares that the Caribbean region's fragmented origins are creating a new, vibrant, unprecedented culture, "a callaloo of ancestral (old) fragments of memory forging a new existential reality."[107] This rhizomatic nature of Caribbean socio-aesthetics is also recognized in Walcott's conversation with Kwame Dawes at the Calabash Literary Festival in 2008. Walcott remarked on the presence of African rhythms in Caribbean literature and poetry, noting their oxymoronic nature, hard as crystals and soft as sponges, stating that "Caribbean aesthetics is 'spongeous,' it absorbs all the influences ..., I think that Caribbean literature has just begun."[108]

The Jamaican economist and professor Norman Girvan, in his keynote address at the St. Martin Book Fair in June 2012, observed essential connections among economics, culture, and major societal change. At a colloquium on "The Caribbean That Unites Us" in Santiago de Cuba in July of the same year, Girvan developed the ideas with a description of Sekou as "a rather extraordinary individual"[109] who embraces multiple roles in his literary, journalistic, historical, cultural, and political activity in St. Martin. Girvan also observed how economics must be entangled with and supported by cultural integration because culture is at the foundation of any major social or socio-aesthetic change:

> I firmly believe that true integration can never be purely or even primarily a matter of economics … the bedrock of integration must be a sense, not so much of common identity—because we do not have identical identities—but what could be called a "community of identities"; identities fashioned in response to a very special historical experience.[110]

This reflection on contemporary Caribbean evades the pressing question of identity and falls within the multicultural expression of voices where Caribbean literature is present as a beautiful music, featuring voices that are audible as solos or flourishes and as part of a large-scale poetic ensemble.

SEKOU'S SOCIO-AESTHETIC FABRIC IN A CARIBBEAN FINE-GRAINED POETIC PANOPLY

> *Ignorance feeds on difference(s).*
> *Harmony fights ignorance.*
>
> – Sara Florian

The title of this work on Lasana M. Sekou, *Caribbean Counterpoint*, hints—in the use of a piece of musical vocabulary—at his poetic voice as both independent from and interdependent with other Caribbean voices. As the voices of the Caribbean have progressively found new renaissances of the arts, this musical term becomes even more appropriate. Counterpoint is the name for a type of music that developed during Europe's Renaissance and the later Baroque period, which consisted in the harmonization of alternating and blending different voices that produced a sense of unity when they were orchestrated together. Likewise, poets of the Caribbean exhibit their own literary contours and colors, but they sing together, expressing different aspects of their society and creating an exquisite, complex poetic ensemble in their production as a whole.

Sekou's voice, arising out of the swamp of St. Martin, his salt marsh, his pond, or climbing and descending the heights with the maroons does not always speak in creole, but he often uses the creole languages of the Caribbean, forms of speech, including his St. Martin *nation tongue* to define his roots and characterize his writing. His voice is polysemic and polyglottic at the same time. His poet-warrior voice is strong, resembling the battle given by the maroons, and it is salty too, salty as unholy Slavery.

In *Aesthetic Theory*, Theodor Adorno affirmed that the individual filters the social work as it is embedded in a work of art. Some consider aesthetics to be characterized of art for art's sake, the philosophical study of pure beauty. Of course, it is more than that, and it surely is not limited to this contextless type of view in Sekou's poetry. Rather, there is also a type of poetics centered around Sekou's messages and literary commitment. Sekou's expression, which often expresses the beauty of living beyond suffering and exploitation and the strength within a people, are revelatory of a continuum to be found in the Caribbean islands, which Brathwaite defined as a submarine unity. Its eruptions in literature are given by the *riddims* of African origin that survived the Middle Passage together with the people who crossed in chains.

These *riddims* may surface as musical genres that pervade writing, as in the work of Sekou, the Trinidadian David Rudder and the Barbadian AJA. They can be shouted from within the text in the form of a socio-political commitment. In this, Sekou's "work seems… to be carrying forward the legacy of Aimé Césaire most forcefully today," according to the Nigerian Professor and Harvard University scholar Francis Abiola Irele in "The Poetic Legacy of Aimé Césaire" (2009). Sekou's work also shares some features here with the Guyanese Martin Carter, the St. Lucian Kendel Hippolyte, the Grenadian Merle Collins, and the Jamaican Joan Andrea Hutchinson. When these poets call for justice, they do so through what is considered "broken English," but it is their mature creoles, with their angular and original rhythms.

The language is the core, Brathwaite's *nam*. Poetry amplifies, in Sekou, many voices that must be heard, starting from the captives chained to the bottom of the slave ships and drowned at sea, described in *The Salt Reaper's* "cradle of the nation," and examined in the heart- and soul-wrenching "forensics" of Sekou's *Book of the Dead* (2016), or the victims of the dreadful hurricanes that are recounted in his *Hurricane Protocol* (2019). In his aesthetics, it is critical for the voices of the maroons and their right to fight for their survival and freedom to be heard, to be recognized. In traditions that are rooted in an oral delivery, as the Afro-Caribbean one is, the poet grants a voice to the folk, founded in an aesthetics of orality, as is the case with the poet Bruce St. John's vernacular work in Bajan.

The economy of Caribbean poetic texts contains other threads, constituted by tropes, craft, philosophy, painting (such as in the case of Earl McKenzie), and spiritual expression. Among these threads is found a cluster of features deriving from what Brathwaite defines as jazz aesthetics, such as poetic flourishes, rhythmical repetitions, and improvisation, as in the poetry of the Vincentian Shake Keane. Sekou's poetry presents all these features and more. It is complete with craft, innovative outlines, musicality, visual play-craft, calligrams, and a creative disposition of words on the page, with powerful performance, imaginative use of metaphor, embroidery of the page, crudity of historical facts, and acridity of political contest.

Society is not perfect, and history shows how much humanity still needs to learn. All these frictions and *embrayages* can be taken on by the poet, invested with a panoply, that is a full armor, to face this fight as "poet-warrior." Nettleford reminds us of the rooting of the Haitian and Cuban revolutions in culture. Similarly, Sekou's extensive and encyclopedic cultural knowledge supports the vector, on which he rides toward a poetic and political revolution, which is extending by osmosis from his own "I-land" to all the Caribbean people of the diaspora, to all Black people, and onward to peoples of all countries and all those suffering from injustices around the world. In Sekou's oeuvre, the St. Martin Salt Reaper invites humanity to a "rendezvous with victory." Glissant speaks of the mangrove's rhizomatic roots, and Sekou's rhizomatic poetry is extending to the rest of the world swamp.

Appendix

The following interview was published in *Tripwire: a journal of poetics* 9 (2015): 113-121. https://tripwirejournal.files.wordpress.com/2014/07/tw9-w_cover.pdf: 115-123.

SARA FLORIAN
"The Polyglot Pride of St. Martin": an interview with Lasana M. Sekou

Sara Florian: As far as I have noticed, there is a very peculiar linguistic situation in St. Maarten. Would you like to comment about this as an introductory remark?

Lasana M. Sekou: Not only do we have all of the languages of the Caribbean spoken in St. Martin[1] by immigrants native to those languages, but an arguably significant number of St. Martin people, native to the island's core culture, are also bilingual or multilingual, at least functionally so. I say "functional" because there is the question of fluency. I think that the multilingual aptitude, as a cultural feature of the St. Martin people, being able to speak between two to five languages, is due in part to the post-Emancipation period when many of our people emigrated throughout the region, and to European metropoles and US cities, looking for work and education. A number of our people, between the late 1800s and 1963 regularly returned home bringing the new languages, the fashion, the music from the countries and territories where they had gone to work, live, and in some instances where they were born. Between 1963 and the early 1970s, a number of St. Martiners returned home to retire, especially from Papiamentu-speaking Aruba and they became very much involved in the society. The wave of immigrants arriving from throughout the Caribbean between the 1970s and 1980s looking for work in the newly booming tourism industry in St. Martin, included descendants of St. Martiners (both parts of the island) fluent in Spanish and Papiamentu and at times some more fluent in Dutch and French than some of their compatriots that they were meeting at home for the first time. The language cross-fertilization is reinforced, with English as the mediating or even the median language, because in the work place, living spaces, places of socialization, and during business transactions people are in a normative contact with each other and do communicate, even to the degree that there are, of late, stress lines relative to that communication, not only between both parts of the island but within each territory that divides the nation. In St. Martin, English as we speak it, has been used island-wide since the 1700s as, what I would call, the "nation tongue."

SF: So is English the official language in St. Martin?

LMS: English is the popular language, it is the *lingua franca* historically of the St. Martin people. In the South, which is a colony of the Netherlands, English is now an official language along with Dutch. That is a development within the last five years, though as a language of instruction English has been used in some of the schools since the 1980s. It is the language of instruction at the University of St. Martin (USM), which was founded in 1989 and is to date the island's only native tertiary institution. In the North, a colony of France, the official language and language of instruction in the schools is French. Nowadays in the North, the schools in particular and generally the official system are reinforcing the language issue and pushing the use of French. Increasing numbers of children speak only, or predominantly French to their parents and to each other. With regard to the St. Martin nation as a whole this could be seen as a point of division, because it harbors ultimately severe problems of communication for the whole St. Martin people, between families and family friends, neighbors and associates, natives and visitors. There are at least two important government officials of the *Collectivité Territoriale de Saint-Martin* that have publicly suggested that the establishment could formally revisit the traditional place of English in the North but there has been no real policy movement in this direction.[2]

SF: The reinforcement of the use of French in the Northern part of the island looks like a counter tendency against the evolution of the use of languages throughout the Caribbean and in the world in general.

LMS: It is indeed. And to me it looks like and is experienced as a reinforcement of colonialism. Notwithstanding the *Collectivité* as a structural change for the French colony in St. Martin in 2007 and, in the South, the constitutional adjustment for the Dutch "island territory" to a more autonomous territory in 2010, St. Martin had been for the longest while what you would call a neglected island by its colonizers. It was not a trading, military or colonial sub-management center or post in the Caribbean region for any of the European countries that controlled the territory during the post-Columbian period. For example, in the post-Emancipation period the colonial sub-centers in the Caribbean region to which St. Martin was attached was Willemstad, Curacao, for the Dutch part and Basseterre, Guadeloupe for the French part of the island. "There is nothing there," was what not only the colonialist rulers might have said, but what was also uttered by some St. Martiners who migrated to and lived in the western and southern Caribbean and beyond during the first half of the 1900s.

SF: It's really interesting what you say about polyglossia and fluency in the Caribbean and especially in St. Martin, and this seems to be indicative of a post-Emancipation aptitude: the necessity to communicate in different languages, but also the importance to combine languages and musical rhythms. [But, something was "there."] St. Martin became the salt island, the island where the main crop was salt, and that is why you often use 'salt' as a major metaphor…

LMS: Yes. It should be natural for the salt metaphor to be present in the literature of St. Martin. Salt was the main crop on the island during the unholy slave period. After the 1848 Emancipation there were minor and infrequent salt harvests well until the early 1960s. As metaphor and as material salt has the experience of curing, preserving, healing. There is a connection to life's sweetness in some cultures. The Yoruba, I am told, have a saying: "May your life be as sweet as salt." It is also intrinsically connected with the exploitation and human suffering of the enslaved ancestors that toiled away in the salt ponds of St. Martin. St. Martiners created and chanted work songs and topical *quimbé* songs as we labored in the salt pans.[3] Blood, sweat and tears were literally shed in the ponds. News and secrets were shared in the wide salted body of water; *petite marronage* and other escapes and acts of sabotage were planned. Parents and children sold to different plantations on- and off-island would meet in this grueling place of forced labor after long forced separations. Social relationships, in spite of the hard labor, were forged in the Great Salt Pond, sweet social relationships. Because of its size, even while salt was being picked in the other salt ponds, the Great Salt Pond demanded most of the enslaved labor from the island. At times, during peak periods of salt reaping bonded labor from surrounding islands were shipped in. To the extent that the enslaved men, women and children were herded off the plantations from both parts of the island to "pick salt" in the salt pans during the salt reaping season for some 200 years, the Great Salt Pond became the cradle of the St. Martin nation. *The Salt Reaper* poems "salt reaping I" and "salt reaping II" are about this double and layered relationship of salt in the history and culture of the St. Martin people and as a recurring expression of the psyche, even if latently so, at the core of the nation. Both poems are sorts of aesthetic extractions from a conversation, a "relate," with a rather beautiful woman from Sucker Garden [district of St. Martin] who worked in the Great Salt Pond as a very young child during the first half of the last century.

SF: I'm thinking of the other islands, Jamaica, Trinidad, Barbados, Cuba, where they basically had plantations of sugar cane, so this metaphor of the sugar and the salt could be a very interesting one. And this ambivalent relationship could be, in my opinion, translated also to the language, I mean between standard languages and Creoles. I cannot speak as a linguist because I am not a linguist, but I think that some definitions could connect separate languages, and especially in the Caribbean whose poets keep using metaphors and interweave languages: there is a kind of unified conception of the languages used in the different territories. Brathwaite spoke of "nation language," that's what poets use to reproduce the language of the people, the language closer to the natural spoken word.

LMS: Indeed, you speak like Brathwaite, he would be proud to hear you. [laugh]

SF: Well, thank you [laugh] I guess you also employ "nation language" in your poetry.

LMS: I use the term "nation tongue," but it is the same concept. In addition to the layered identification with or deconstruction of the European languages spoken in the region, there is too a sweet fluency to the languages that we created in the Caribbean from the disparate and Calibanic tongues. For example, when you hear someone speaking Papiamentu or Haitian it is just a sweet sound, the way it rolls off the tongue, fluent, fluid…

SF: I would like to slightly shift back to the subject of your own poetry. Apart from the subject and metaphor of salt in your work, you also speak of political issues.

LMS: Indeed. The subjects of politics, history and race are consistently and variedly discussed in all of the literatures of the Caribbean. Salt is linked to culture and history in St. Martin in a unique or specific way as we discussed previously. History is both our bane and the bountiful reservoir of our victories. The political issues I tend to prefer to work with or work out in the poetry tend toward liberation politics, national and human liberation processes in the Caribbean: from slavery, racism, colonialism, neocolonialism and as continuing processes in the region's countries to realize full sovereignty and in the still colonized territories like St. Martin to become independent. When I use political terms and discuss certain political ideas in poetry it is not always related to colonialism. Our nation is one of the last remaining colonies in the region, a physical remnant of a history of horror. Our island of 37 square miles is held captive by Dutch and French colonialism through structures and processes based in part on what Edward Said calls "structures of attitude and reference" and what George Lamming terms a "terror of the mind." Such a terror it is that there are many among us who believe that St. Martin is not a colony but in the South, an "equal partner in the Dutch kingdom," and in the North "*est la France.*" For a colonized people, once enslaved by their colonizers, this is delusional thinking on a grand scale.

SF: Does political terminology have much importance in your poetic production? How do you cope with all these different languages?

LMS: The historical and contemporary political realities in the Caribbean are very important to the poetic language that I work with; words and terms are drawn freely from the region's languages as symbolic of ideals, practices, and manifestation of Caribbean unity – and also as literary devices and elements of exploration of a St. Martin aesthetics. Politics, language, history, religion, the geographic landscape are just a few of the elements I work with to construct a poetry that would hopefully have meaning in the lives of people. In a five-minute communication event, two people in St. Martin can go through up to five languages, seamlessly. As previously noted, this is more of a functional reality than a matter of fluency, but it is certainly a feature of sophistication of the St. Martin people's culture. However, relative the stress signs alluded to earlier, this language culture is not yet an official reality, our politicians and educators are not great advocates of the language culture as it is felt, as it should be owned, even as a natural resource. Arguably the polyglot pride of St. Martin is embattled, there are public, vocal stress signs like never before since the beginning of modern St. Martin. The nation tongue is historically English for both parts of the island, and it has been serving as the median language of unity, communication and business for the people of St. Martin for most of the Survivalist Period (1648-1848), for the Traditional Period (1848-1963) and in the Modern Period (1963-). Mind you, this is not to advocate or favor one European or colonial language over another, but the claim of an English derived from the historical and cultural experiences at the very core of the St. Martin identity. This nation tongue or nation language has been historically imparted to folks who have immigrated and contributed to and become part of the St. Martin nation, even as it is evolving. While the language allegiances of the territorial *governments* are to Dutch in the South and French in the North, most of the island's media and commerce are conducted in

English. The nation's seminal literature is in English but the colonial languages are the languages of instruction in most of the island's schools. The schools in the South with English as the language of instruction have increased significantly since the 1980s, with telling successes. The French educational system has been over a corresponding period, reinforcing French and all things of France in the schools in the North. It should be noted too that as of the late 1980s, boosted by *défiscalisation*, there started what has become a significant settlement of French metropolitans in the North. With that development have also come related charges about racism, language complexes about who is really speaking French, identity issues about who belong in the French territory, economic disparities and displacement between Black St. Martiners and the white metropolitan French, and of late what is for St. Martin an unprecedented tension between gendarmes and the youth. All of these, let's call them elements, have been working their way into the poetic production and projection, from *Born Here* (1986) to *37 Poems* (2005). The linguistic challenges have been best articulated to date in Dr. Rhoda Arrindell's book, *Language, Culture, and Identity in St. Martin* (2014).

—This is an updated version of an interview previously published in *SX Small Axe—a Caribbean platform of criticism.*

---

[1] Sekou uses the traditional or what he calls the nationalist spelling of St. Martin to refer to the entire island, instead of the Dutch spelling of

St. Maarten for the Dutch part in the South and the French spelling of Saint-Martin for the French part in the North.

[2] The Collectivity of St. Martin came into being on 15 July 2007 and encompasses the northern part of the island, which is a French Overseas Collectivity, Collectivité d'Outre-Mer. The St. Maarten Territory, with increased autonomy for the southern part of the island, which is a Dutch territory, came into being on 10 October 2010.

[3] Topical St. Martin song, sung in a fast-paced singsong without musical accompaniment (sung up to mid-20th c.).

© 2008, 2009, 2015 by Sara Florian/Lasana M. Sekou

Endnotes

[1] *Cf.* "Commentary" by Armando Lampe, Ph.D. to *Mothernation—Poems from 1984 to 1987. ix*; Fergus: "In these still colonial territories, art for art's sake is a luxury we cannot afford all the time. For Sekou, poets are absolutely essential to life." Fergus, Howard A. *Love Labor Liberation in Lasana Sekou.* 60.

[2] *Cf.* "Lasana Slideshow Tribute" video at https://youtu.be/wRfVgINQheg.

[3] Lasana Mwanza Sekou changed his name from Harold Hermano Lake while living in New York City. He provided the following information upon my request: "I changed my name in the mid-to-late-1970s, in high school, while working on the poems that would become the manuscript of 'Moods for Isis...' (1978). I can remember thinking that if I could work at becoming a good writer, I wanted an African name as an author to be on my books. By then I knew how Blacks in the Americas/Caribbean had come to lose their/our original names, so there was also, clearly impressed (in my teen head at that time), the issue of claim and re-claiming ('Sekou' was selected because of its meaning as much as because it was from the region where my maternal great great-great-grandmother, Candace, came from, the Guinea). Of course I could have been/must have been influenced by the folks who had changed their names from Euro names to African names during the 1960s/early 1970s—and the militancy relative to that process & stand (I had already been reading some of the writers who had changed their names, e.g. Amiri Baraka) but the writer's reason and claim were foremost and I can still remember thinking it. (…); Lasana = poet (East African, though I am told it is a version of the West African 'Lansana' but I have no concrete evidence); Mwanza = wise protector (Central Africa); Sekou = warrior (West

Africa; I have been told since that it is a version of 'sheikh' but again I have not read/did not pursue for evidence)." Personal communication with the poet. E-mail. 6 July 2012. See also Askhari Hodari, Ph.D. *The African Book of Names*. Deerfield Beach, Florida: HCI: 2009: Lasana or 'lah-SAH-nah' means poet (East Africa), 306. Mwanza or 'mwah-zah' means wise protector (Central Africa), 220. Sekou means fighter or warrior (West Africa), 19.

[4] "The 37-square mile island is in actual fact divided between the Dutch and the French. The Dutch spelling 'Sint Maarten' was adopted in 1946, as a way of the colonialists claiming the 'Dutchness' of the part of the island that falls directly under Dutch rule. Before then, the whole island was referred to as 'Saint Martin' which is also the French spelling of the name purportedly given to the island by Christopher Columbus. (...) The official Dutch spelling however remains 'St. Maarten.'" Badejo, Fabian Adekunle. "Modern Literature in English in the Dutch Windward Islands: A Brief Introduction." *Calabash: A Journal of Caribbean Arts and Letters* 1.2 (Spring-Summer 2002): 77. I will hereafter adopt the spelling of St. Martin. With regard to the Amerindian names for the island, "Sualouiga, Öualichi (Sualouiga), also pronounced and written Souliaga or Soualiga, is thought to be an Island Carib word meaning 'Land of Salt.' Öualichi, also pronounced and written Qualichi, is said to be an Arawakan word meaning 'Land of Women' or 'Land of Brave Women.'" Sekou, Lasana M. *National Symbols of St. Martin—A Primer*. 3.

[5] Walcott, Derek. "A Sea-Chantey," *In a Green Night: Poems 1948-1960*. 46.

[6] Lampe, Armando. "Por la aparición de Double Play." *Revista Mexicana del Caribe*, Vol. V, Núm. 010, 2000. 240.

⁷ Houat, Louis Timagène. *Les marrons*. rééd. By Metinger, Serge, and J.C. Carpanin. Océan Indien: Madagascar, La Réunion, Maurice. 456.

⁸ Sekou, Lasana. *Nativity and monologues for today*. Glossary. 73.

⁹ *Cf.* Sekou, Lasana. *National Symbols of St. Martin*. 107.

¹⁰ *Cf.* Castiglioni, L., Mariotti, S. *Vocabolario della lingua latina*. Milano: Loescher Editore, 1990. 931.

¹¹ *Cf.* Rocci, Lorenzo. *Vocabolario greco-italiano*. Città di Castello: Società Editrice Dante Alighieri, 1993. 79.

¹² *Cf.* "The importance of salt," 1999. http://mygeologypage.ucdavis.edu/cowen/~gel115/salt.html; SI, Salt Institute, "Salt in European history." http://www.saltinstitute.org/Uses-benefits/Salt-in-history/Salt-in-modern-history/Europe, 2011; and "Salt works," http://www.saltworks.us/salt_info/si_HistoryOfSalt.asp, 2011. 17 July 2012.

¹³ *Cf.* Speaking of the Gospel of Matthew, I'd like to add the Latin quotation: "vos estis sal terrae. quod si evaneruit, in quo salietur? ad nihil valet ultra, nisi ut mittatur foras, et conculcetur ob hominibus." (5:13, *Vulgate*)

¹⁴ Fergus, Howard A. *Love Labor Liberation in Lasana Sekou*. 135.

¹⁵ *Cf.* "il testo è sempre un «futuro anteriore»: eco e precursore, fuori tempo, urto fra «prima» e «dopo»." Kristeva, Julia. "Lo stato e il mistero." *La rivoluzione del linguaggio poetico*. 350. *Cf.* De Caroli, Maria Elvira. *Una briglia all'emozione. Creatività e psicoanalisi*. Miano: Franco Angeli, 2002. 146.

¹⁶ "… la plantación tuvo formas de manifestarse no siempre asociadas al cultivo de la caña de azúcar. (…) Desde el primer tercio del siglo XVII se detectó la importancia de las Salinas que fueron localizadas allí." Emilio Jorge Rodríguez, "Plantación salina y convivencia regional: la poética de Lasana M. Sekou."

El Caribe literario, Trazados de convivencia. La Habana, Arte y Literatura, 2011. 135; *Cf.* Menkman, W.R. *De Nederlanders in het Caraibische Zeegebied waarin vervat de Geschiedenis der Nederlandsche Antillen*. 39.

[17] Sekou, Lasana M. "Great Salt Pond Speaks." *The Salt Reaper – poems from the flats*. 35.

[18] *Cf.* Castiglioni, L., Mariotti, S. *Vocabolario della lingua latina*. Milano: Loescher Editore, 1990. 928.

[19] *Cf.* Rocci, Lorenzo. *Vocabolario greco-italiano*. Città di Castello: Società Editrice Dante Alighieri, 1993. 1651.

[20] Fiorani, Flavio, e Marcello Flores. *Storia Illustrata dei Grandi Imperi Coloniali*. 115. It is noteworthy that until XVIII c. half of Europe's refineries were centered in Amsterdam. See also "Slavery shaped the West Indies. It was expensive and inconvenient, and presented considerable problems of governance; but nobody came up with an alternative, especially for the production of sugar." Chamberlin, J. Edward. *Come back to me my language—Poetry and the West Indies*. 1.

[21] Lamming, George. *Coming, Coming Home—Conversations II*. 7.

[22] Interview with Lasana M. Sekou, 15 May 2008, Philipsburg, St. Maarten.

[23] Dijkhoff, Marta, Dr. *Sweet Salt—contemporary & classical steel pan music by Neville York*. Audio CD. Liner notes. 3.

[24] Baly, Camille E. *Ibid*. CD sleeve. 3.

[25] "S'Maatin Then and Now! A historic and photographic excursion." http://www.stmaartenlibrary.org/"s'maatin-then-and-now-historic-and-photographic-excursion.

[26] Fergus, Howard A. *Love Labor Liberation in Lasana Sekou*. 44.

[27] Interview with Lasana M. Sekou, 15 May 2008, Philipsburg, St. Maarten. *Cf.* Sekou, Lasana. *National Symbols of St. Martin.* 113.

[28] Sekou, Lasana M. *The Salt Reaper—poems from the flats. iv.*

[29] Cooper, Carolyn. "*The Salt Reaper: Poems from the flats* by Lasana M. Sekou" by Mary Hanna. Book review. *Caribbean Quarterly* (Vol. 55, No. 1, March 2009).

[30] Sekou, Lasana. *National Symbols of St. Martin.* 6.

[31] Sekou, Lasana M. *The Salt Reaper—poems from the flats.* 36.

[32] Clarke writes in the epilogue, as also Gilkes acknowledges, that the title of DDIH derives from "a dream in which he addressed in the streets of a 'desolate city' by a derelict rummaging through garbage bins." Gilkes, Michael. "A True Space. A commentary on LeRoy Clarke's 'De Distance is Here'." *De Distance Is Here. The El Tucuche Poems 1984-2007.* 20.

[33] Taylor, Jeremy and Lee, Simon. "Warrior Art." 50-56.

[34] "Think of a pyramid, with two feet at the bases. Fragments of a Spiritual under the left foot, Douens under the right. The pyramid acquires two shoulders, as the poet develops new phases. In *De Maze: A Single Line to My Soul* deals with Man's choices and the decision to overcome distraction. One of the paintings *"Under It All, I All Right"* shows the poet under stress, beset by drugs and confusion and dreadness, but looking into a clear pool, which could be his tears, and the reflection is pure, the face is clear. On the opposite shoulder, Eye Am (...) *El Tucuche Approaching Apotheosis: The Divining of Man.* Man looks across from El Tucuche from his new height, and sees what is higher still: Aripo. He is stunned by what he sees; a brief ecstatic vision of unity." Clarke, LeRoy. "LeRoy Clarke."

[35] Houat, Louis Timagène. *Les marrons.* rééd. By Metinger, Serge, and J.C. Carpanin. Océan Indien: Madagascar, La Réunion, Maurice. 461.

[36] Sekou, Lasana M. *The Salt Reaper—poems from the flats*. 35.

[37] Fergus, Howard A. *Love Labor Liberation in Lasana Sekou*. x.

[38] Jack, Deborah Drisana. "Unearthing Memories: A Conversation with St. Martin Artist Deborah Jack." Interview by Jacqueline Bishop. *Calabash: A Journal of Caribbean Arts and Letters* (Volume 2, Number 2: Summer/Fall 2003). 87-107.

[39] *Cf.* Florian, Sara. "The quest for roots: Sekou's *Brotherhood of the Spurs* and the search for a St. Martin identity." *Moko magazine*. Issue 14. Nov. 2018. http://mokomagazine.org/wordpress/the-quest-for-roots-sekous-brotherhood-of-the-spurs-and-the-search-for-a-st-martin-identity/.

[40] Jack, Deborah. "Feature – In Conversation with Deborah Jack for SITElines: Unsettled Landscapes." Interview by Tiana Reid. *ARC Magazine* (1 Sept. 2014). http://arcthemagazine.com/arc/2014/09/in-conversation-with-deborah-jack-for-sitelines-unsettled-landscapes/

[41] Sekou, Lasana. "forensics." *Book of the Dead*. 43. *Cf.* also Florian, Sara. Review of Lasana M. Sekou's *The Book of the Dead*. *Tripwire: a journal of poetics*, 15, Buuck, David, ed., Oakland, California: Bookmobile, 2019. Forthcoming.

[42] Sekou, Lasana. "Labrish." *Book of the Dead*. 5.

[43] Sekou, Lasana M. "the house we are building." *Mothernation – Poems from 1984 to 1987*. 46.

[44] The 'blès' is described by Donatien-Yssa as "une maladie non reconnue par la médecine occidentale, qui, dans la Caraïbe, touche essentiellement les jeunes sujets. Affection psychosomatique ou imaginaire, elle peut prendre la forme de désordres physiques, mais elle peut également atteindre les fonctions mentales de l'individu et se manifester sous forme de confusions allant d'une mélancolie sans conséquence jusqu'à des troubles graves altérant la santé physique et mentale du sujet. Cette affection se serait développée au cours des quatre siècles

d'esclavage et de colonisation, suite aux souffrances endurées par les générations successives de Caribéens." Donatien-Yssa, Patricia. "Leroy Clarke: The Double Ritual of Poetic and Plastic Creation, a Way to Freedom / Leroy Clarke entre Poésie et Peinture, Chantre de la Spiritualité et de la Liberté." 85.

[45] *Cf.* Clarke, LeRoy. "Voice of a Smouldering Coal…" 10 July 2009. Article sent by the poet. Personal communication with the poet. E-mail. 4 Nov. 2009.

[46] Fergus, Howard A. "Lasana M. Sekou. *Love Songs Make You Cry*." Book review. *The Caribbean Writer* (Volume 4, 1990). 100.

[47] *Ibid.*

[48] Debien, Gabriel. "Le marronage." *Les esclaves aux Antilles françaises (XVIIe-XVIIIe siècles)*. 411.

[49] *Ibid.* 456-7.

[50] *Cf.* Rochmann, Marie-Christine. *L'esclave fugitif dans la littérature antillaise*.

[51] *Ibid.* 252.

[52] *Ibid.* 388.

[53] Sekou, Lasana M. *Nativity / Nativité / Natividad—Trilingual Edition*. 37.

[54] "*rammagé*," also spelled "*ramajé.*" *Cf.* Allsopp, Richard. *Dictionary of Caribbean English Usage*, OUP, 1996 and UWI Press, 2003: "'*ramajé*' could mean 'to play an impromptu composition on steelpan,' from French Creole '*ramager*' '[of birds] to chirp, to warble.'" 465.

[55] Badejo, Fabian A. *Revolution as Poetic Inspiration: Grenada in 'Maroon Lives' by Lasana Sekou*.

[56] I would like to thank Lasana Sekou for sharing with me these observations. Personal communication with the poet. May 2008. E-mail. 16 Jan. 2010.

[57] The theme of remnants of lost languages coming from the primitive voice of Amerindians is analysed by Régis Antoine in "Paroles perdues de l'Indien et du nègre marron." 13-33.

[58] I would like to thank Sekou for this observation: "*'veuglé, sa çe bois'* means 'dazzled, this is wood,' it's a kind of an exclamation in kweyol (I believe St. Lucian but probably in other kweyols too). The word 'wood' is a phallic symbol reference/a sexual connotation, which for the poem, lends itself to the sweetness of copulation (engaging the truth / essence / union etc. of life) / pregnancy / birth... thus the subsequent line 'children at the window witnessing their own birth' (this poem / line influenced the cover art for *Quimbé*)." Personal communication with the poet. E-mail. 28 Dec. 2009.

[59] Sekou uses this same expression in the collection of short stories *Love Songs Make You Cry* (1989) when one of the two protagonists, a young woman, said: "'The women of my country are treated like nothing in *San Martin, San materialismo*'." Sekou, Lasana M. "Love Songs Make You Cry." *Love Songs Make You Cry*. 84.

[60] In this re-writing of Sekou's lines the expressions in German will be translated into English: "the afro-look / of the Black German (This is a typo, "Deutschen" confirmed by the poet, "schwarzen Deutschen" means the "Black German." Personal communication with the poet. E-mail. 12 Oct. 2009.) / and immigrant people all (...) / and distant lands (...) / what power does not is what you will not / you are true sun children (...) / this is the spirit of the time (...) / listen racist motherfuckers (...) / in the mirror [*Der Spiegel* is also the title of a German magazine," NbR] of inwardly brutalized / races / this ain' no dibi-dibi "atomic power" / pinned down on its back / listen all, listen at all time, listen everybody, / the victory in unity" (*Quimbé*, 101).

⁶¹ Badejo, Fabian Adekunle. *Salted Tongues—Modern Literature in St.Martin*. 44.

⁶² "virtually all the languages spoken in the Caribbean can be heard on St. Martin, St. Martiners themselves are not really polyglots even though they are often multi-lingual. They normally speak English at home, study in Dutch (or French) at school, and often socialize in Spanish and/or Papiamento." *Ibid.* 76.

⁶³ *Cf.* "the poet's nation language has been influenced by Brathwaite known for his 'video style' writing (...) These stylistic devices began as early as *Mothernation* and *Quimbé* in 1991." Fergus, Howard A. *Love Labor Liberation in Lasana Sekou*. 128.

⁶⁴ Brathwaite, Kamau. *Islands*. 72.

⁶⁵ Brathwaite, Kamau. "The Dust." *Rights of Passage. The Arrivants*. 66.

⁶⁶ *Cf.* Nowak, Mark. "Labor Love."

⁶⁷ Fergus, Howard A. *Ibid.* 129.

⁶⁸ The acronyms are decoded as follows: "bdt": British Dependent Territories; "bot": British Overseas Territories; "bvi": British Virgin Islands; "bwi": British West Indies; "cpr": Commonwealth of Puerto Rico; "dc": Dutch Caribbean; "dwi": Dutch West Indies; "fod": French Overseas Department; "fwi": French West Indies; "na": Netherlands Antilles; "upt": Ultra-Peripheral Territory; "usvi": US Virgin Islands; "dom-tom": Départments d'outre-mer and Térritoires d'outre-mer.

⁶⁹ For an in-depth study of the Dread Talk *Cf.* Velma Pollard's *Dread Talk*.

⁷⁰ "The up-to-date *37 Poems* with its polished journalistic tone does not eschew the people's language. The book generally features China, but the St. Martin poems in the collection reflect island rhythms and realities". Fergus, Howard A. *Love Labor Liberation in Lasana Sekou*. 124.

[71] "The collection begins with a trilingual description of a Sunday "mass" (weekly picnic-like gathering of immigrant domestic workers) in Hong Kong and contains the political poems." Khair, Tabish. "Introduction: Reasons to Live." Sekou, Lasana M. *37 Poems*. x.

[72] I would like to thank Lasana for this observation. Personal communication with the poet. E-mail. 12 Oct. 2009.

[73] The "onyx eyes" (33) of "beijing monday." *37 Poems.*

[74] "The critic Tabish Kahir recognized that in his introduction to *37 Poems* when he insists that "xinXin," penned in China, is essentially a love poem." Fergus, Howard A. *Love Labor Liberation in Lasana Sekou*. 14.

[75] Offshore Editing Service. "Angelo Rombley Music Mix for Lasana Sekou's First Poetry-Music CD, Launch Nov. 8 2008." Personal communication with the poet. E-mail by House of Nehesi Publishers. 7 Oct. 2008.

[76] Clark, Fernando R. *The Salt Reaper—selected poems from the flats*. Audio CD. Liner notes. 5.

[77] Baraka, Amiri. *The Salt Reaper—selected poems from the flats*. Audio CD. Liner notes. 1.

[78] Winks, Christopher. Book review. "Lasana M. Sekou. *Nativity / Nativité / Natividad*." *Caribbean Vistas Journal:* Critiques of *Caribbean Arts and Cultures*. 2 Apr. 2014. http://caribbeanvistas.files.wordpress.com/2014/04/nativity-nativitecc81-natividad.pdf.

[79] *Cf.* Sekou, Lasana M. "Great Salt Pond Speaks." *The Salt Reaper—poems from the flats*. 36.

[80] Fergus, Howard A. *Love Labor Liberation in Lasana Sekou*. 60.

[81] *Ibid.* 85; Nowak, Mark. "Labor Love."; Badejo, Fabian Adekunle. *Salted Tongues*. xi.

[82] James, Conrad M., Dr. "St. Martin Writer Releases Book Of New Poetry." http://www.stkittsgazette.com/st-martin-writer-releases-book-of-new-poetry/. 24 Sept. 2010.

[83] My translation of "Cette mosaïque linguistique, en constant évolution vers plus d'harmonie, de clarté, de pureté et de finesse dans l'ortographe purement phonétique et dans la pronunciation, donnera naissance à toute une literature extrêmement pittoresque, vivante, imagée mais sourtout orale." Morpeau, Louis. "La Muse Haïtienne d'Expression Créole." 18.

[84] Keane, E. McG. "Some Religious Attitudes in W.I. Poetry. The Orthodox Attitude and Variations." 169.

[85] Dathorne, O.R., ed. *Caribbean Verse, An Anthology*. 11.

[86] *Cf.* the 1957 Walcott's article, "Society and the Artist."

[87] Perse, St.-John. "Poésie/On Poetry." Speech of Acceptance upon the Award of the Nobel Prize for Literature. 9.

[88] "the poet also is tied to historical events." *Ibid.* 11

[89] "When Derek Walcott said that 'West Indian literature originated in verse' he was only stating a half truth. What has happened is that the West Indian novel […] emanated from poets and therefore remained 'poetic' in form and language." Dathorne, O.R., ed. *Caribbean Verse, An Anthology*. 1.

[90] Figueroa, John J.M., ed. *Caribbean Voices. An Anthology of West Indian Poetry*. Vol. 1. 11.

[91] Lewis, Sir Arthur. "On Being Different. The Graduation Address delivered at the U.W.I., Cave Hill, Barbados, on 5th February, 1971." 8.

[92] Rohlehr, Gordon. Personal communication with the scholar. E-mail. 22 Oct. 2008. *Cf.* also "Eric Roach, for example, reviewed *Savacou ¾* in Trinidad Guardian. Restricting his commentary to an examination of some of the poetry, Mr. Roach described his criteria for determining what was art, and what was good and bad poetry. In so doing, he joined a sharp debate which is going

on about aesthetics, tradition, literary criticism and sensibility in the West Indies." Rohlehr, Gordon. "West Indian Poetry: Some Problems of Assessment. Part Two." 109.

[93] Personal communication with Wayne Brown. E-mail. 9 Nov. 2008.

[94] "L'histoire de la poésie antillaise suit étroitement celle de l'évolution de la société." Condé, Maryse, ed. *La Poésie Antillaise*. 4.

[95] *Ibid*. 5.

[96] "L'Antillanité a principalement pour théoricien le poète-romancier Edouard Glissant.[...] Le rôle du poète, de l'écrivain plus généralment, est de travailler à la guérison de sa communauté d'abord en analysant soigneusement les causes de ce mal, puis en tentant de proposer des solutions. [...] L'Antillanité naîtra après la Libération des Antilles, ou si l'on préfère la fin de la dépedance culturelle et politique dans laquelle elles se trouvent." *Ibid*. 70-1.

[97] Glissant, Édouard. *Le discours antillais*. Paris: Éditions du Seuil, 1981. 230.

[98] Glissant, Édouard. *Caribbean Discourse. Selected Essays*. xii.

[99] *Cf*. For another employment of the myth of Orpheus, see Florian, Sara. "Review of Earl McKenzie's Ernest Palmer's Dream and Other Stories." *Bookends. The Sunday Observer*. 22 July 2018. 4.

[100] Brathwaite, Edward Kamau. *History of the Voice*. 16.

[101] Carter, Martin. "The Location of the Artist." (1979) *University of Hunger*. 232-4.

[102] Rohlehr, Gordon. "Articulating a Caribbean Aesthetic: The Revolution of Self-Perception." (1979) *My Strangled City and Other Essays*. 1-2.

[103] Aiyejina, Funso. "Derek Walcott: The Poet as a Federated Consciousness." *World Literature Written in English* 27.1 (Spring 1987): 78.

[104] Interview with Lasana M. Sekou. 15 May 2008.

[105] Badejo, Fabian Adekunle. *Salted Tongues*. 68.

[106] Nettleford, Rex. "The Caribbean's Creative Diversity: the Defining Point of the region's History." Lecture delivered by Prof. Rex Nettleford, Vice Chancellor, University of the West Indies. University of Guyana, Guyana. 21 Mar. 2003. Press Release 54/2003. 4 Apr. 2003.

[107] Sekou, Lasana M. "Color & Cultural Identity: A Caribbean Story." (Keynote Address by Lasana M. Sekou, 10 annual Caribbean "Islands-In-Between" Conference, St. Martin, 2007). https://youtu.be/xDABGPoH34s.

[108] Walcott, Derek. "Derek Walcott in conversation with Kwame Dawes." Calabash Literary Festival. 24 May 2008.

[109] Girvan, Norman. "Caribbean integration: can cultural production succeed where politics and economics have failed? (Confessions of a Wayward Economist)." Posted on 15 July 2012. 7.

[110] *Ibid.*

Bibliography

Works by and on Sekou

Sekou, Lasana M. *37 Poems*. St. Martin: House of Nehesi Publishers, 2005.

_____. *Big Up. St Martin Essay & Poem.* "Colony, Territory, or Partner?" "The Cubs Are in the Field." St. Martin: House of Nehesi Publishers, 1999.

_____. *Book of the Dead*. St. Martin: House of Nehesi Publishers, 2016.

_____. *Born Here*. St. Maarten: House of Nehesi. 1986.

_____. "CasualtiesFX3." Casualties Music Video from *The Salt Reaper—selected poems from the flats*. by Angelo Rombley. Big Eye Opener Studios, 2009. YouTube. 24 Aug. 2009 http://www.youtube.com/watch?v= JlWWBMWPs7c.

_____. "Color & Cultural Identity: A Caribbean Story." Keynote Address, 10th Annual Eastern Caribbean Islands' Cultures Conference, "The Islands In Between." Proc. of a conference. Nov. 1-4 2007. Philipsburg Community & Cultural Center, Philipsburg. St. Martin: House of Nehesi Publishers.

_____. "Eterno Tiempo de Siembra." 2004. Memoria Audio-visual del Festival Internacional de Poesía de Medellín. Poetas de América. Online video. 10 Oct. 2009 http://www.festivaldepoesiademedellin.org/pub.php/es/Multimedia/sekou.htm.

_____. *Fête. Celebrating St. Martin's Traditional Festive Music. Revised Edition.* St. Martin: House of Nehesi Publishers. 2008.

_____. "Final Roughneck." Music Video from *The Salt Reaper—selected poems from the flats*. by Angelo Rombley. Big Eye Opener Studios, 2009. YouTube. 3 Sept. 2012 http://www.youtube.com/watch?v=Hvq8jb_yHqM.

_____. *For the Mighty Gods… An Offering*. PDF file sent by the author via e-mail. 20 Aug. 2008. New York: House of Nehesi, 1982.

_____. *Hurricane Protocol*. St. Martin: House of Nehesi Publishers, 2019.

_____."Lasana M. Sekou." Website. House of Nehesi Publishers 15 May 2008. http://www.houseofnehesipublish.com/sekou.html.

_____. *Love Songs Make You Cry*. St. Maarten: House of Nehesi, 1989.

_____. *Maroon Lives—for Grenadian freedom fighters*. PDF file sent by the author via e-mail. 13 Aug. 2008. New York: House of Nehesi, 1983.

_____. *Moods for Isis—Picture poems of Love & Struggle*. PDF file sent by the author via e-mail. 17 Aug. 2008. Self-published. New York: Black News Typographers, 1978.

_____. *Mothernation—Poems from 1984 to 1987*. St. Maarten: House of Nehesi, 1991.

_____, ed. *National Symbols of St. Martin. A Primer*. St. Martin: House of Nehesi Publishers, 1997.

_____. *Nativity and monologues for today*. St. Maarten: House of Nehesi, 1988.

_____. "Poetry Reading." 3 Dec. 1986. CD-ROM. Radio Unit, Mona, Jamaica. <n. d.> Courtesy of the Library of the Spoken Word, University of the West Indies, Mona, Jamaica.

_____. *Quimbé—The Poetics of Sound*. St. Maarten: House of Nehesi, 1991.

_____. ed. *The Independence Papers. Readings on a New Political Status for St. Maarten/St. Martin, Volume 1*. St. Maarten: House of Nehesi, 1990.

_____. *The Salt Reaper—poems from the flats*. St. Martin: House of Nehesi Publishers, 2005.

_____. *The Salt Reaper—selected poems from the flats*. CD-ROM. House of Nehesi Publishers. Record Label: Mountain Dove Records. 2009. 24 Aug. 2009 http://www.cdbaby.com/cd/lasanamsekou.

Works consulted

Adorno, Theodor W. *Aesthetic Theory*. Eds. Gretel Adorno, and Rolf Tiedemann. Trans. C. Lenhardt. London: Routledge and Kegan Paul, 1984.

Allen-Agostini, Lisa. "S'maatin poems." *The Caribbean Review of Books*. Feb. 2006. www.meppublishers.com.

Allsopp, Jeannette. *The Caribbean Multilingual Dictionary of Flora, Fauna and Foods in English, French, French Creole and Spanish*. Kingston, Jamaica: Arawak Publications, 2003.

Allsopp, Richard. *Dictionary of Caribbean English Usage*. Oxford: OUP, 1996; Mona, Jamaica: University of the West Indies Press, 2003.

Andwele, Adisa Jelani (ÀJA). *All as 1*. CD-ROM. Caribbean Records (Barbados) Ltd. Ashdeane Village, Black Rock, St. Michael, Barbados. 2008.

_____. *Antiquity*. Leeds: Peepal Tree Press, 2002.

_____. *Don't Let Me Die. Perspective, Poems & Photographs on War & Poverty and Their Impact on Children*. Rock Hall, St. Thomas, Barbados: Adisa Andwele, 2002.

Aiyejina, Funso. "Derek Walcott: The Poet as a Federated Consciousness." *World Literature Written in English*, 27.1 (Spring 1987): 67-80. Modern Language Association of America and University of Guelph, Ontario, Canada.

"Angelo Rombley Music Mix for Lasana Sekou's First Poetry-Music CD, Launch Nov. 8 2008." *St. Maarten Island Time.com*. 6 Oct. 2008. 4 Aug. 2009 http://www.sxmislandtime.

com/index.php?option=com_content&view=article&id=3407%3Aangelo-rombley-music-mix-for-lasana-sekous-first-poetry-music-cd-launch-nov-8&Itemid=77.

Antoine, Régis. "Paroles perdues de l'Indien et du nègre marron." *La littérature Franco-Antillaise (Haïti, Guadeloupe, Martinique)*. Paris: Kartala, 1992. 13-33.

Askhari Hodari, Ph.D. *The African Book of Names*. Deerfield Beach, Florida: HCI, 2009.

Badejo, Fabian Adekunle. "Introduction." Edward Kamau Brathwaite. *Words Need Love Too*. St. Martin: House of Nehesi Publishers, 2000. *ix-xx*.

_____. "Modern Literature in English in the Dutch Windward Islands: A Brief Introduction." *Calabash: A Journal of Caribbean Arts and Letters* 1.2 (Spring-Summer 2001): 65-77. Eds. Jacqueline Bishop, Michela Calderaro. New York: New York University. 5 May 2009 http://www.nyu.edu/calabash/.

_____. "Revolution as Poetic Inspiration: Grenada in 'Maroon Lives' by Lasana Sekou." Paper presented at the IXth Annual Conference of the Caribbean Studies Association, St. Kitts, May 29 – June 2, 1984.

_____. *Salted Tongues—Modern Literature in St.Martin*. St. Martin: House of Nehesi Publishers, 2003.

Baraka, Amiri. *Funk Lore, New Poems (1984-1995)*. Ed. Paul Vangelisti. Los Angeles: Littoral Books, 1996.

Baugh, Edward. "A History of Poetry." Ed. James A. Arnold. *A History of Literature in the Caribbean. Vols. 2*. Amsterdam: John Benjamin, 2001. 227-282.

Benìtez-Rojo, Antonio. *The Repeating Island. The Caribbean and the Postmodern Perspective*. Trans. James Maraniss. Durham and London: Duke UP, 2001. Or. title *La Isla que se Repite: El Caribe y la Perspective Postmoderna*. Barcelona, Spain: Editorial Casiopea, 1989.

Benveniste, Emile. *Il Vocabolario delle Istituzioni Indoeuropee. Vols. 1 and 2*. Ed. Mariantonia Liborio. Torino: Einaudi, 2001; 1976 (Or. title Paris: Les Editions de Minuit, 1969).

Brathwaite, Edward Kamau. *Ancestors*. New York: New Directions Books, 2001.

―――. *Barabajan Poems, 1492-1992*. Kingston; New York: Savacou North; Kingston, Jamaica: Savacou Publications, 1994.

―――. *Black + Blues*. New York: New Directions Publishing, 1995.

―――. *Born to Slow Horses*. Middletown, Connecticut, Wesleyan University Press, 2005.

―――. "Dream Orange." *The Caribbean Writer* 9 (1995): 117-134. Eds. Marvin E. Williams and Erika J. Waters. University of the Virgin Islands. 5 May 2005 http://www.thecaribbeanwriter.org/toc/tocvolume9.html.

―――. "History, the Caribbean writer and X/Self." Eds. Geoffrey V. Davis and Hena Maes-Jelinek. *Crisis and Creativity in the New Literatures in English*. Amsterdam: Rodopi, 1990.

―――. *History of the Voice, The Development of Nation Language in Anglophone Caribbean Poetry*. London; Port of Spain: New Beacon Books, 1984.

―――. *Islands*. London: Oxford University Press, 1969.

―――. *Masks*. Oxford: Oxford University Press, 1968.

―――. *Mother Poem*. Oxford; New York: Oxford UP, 1977.

―――. *Namsetoura & the Companion Stranger*. http://anthurium.miami.edu/volume_1/issue_1/brathwaite-namsetoura.htm.

―――. *Other Exiles*. New York; Toronto: Oxford UP, 1975.

―――. *Sappho Sakyi's Meditations*. Mona, Jamaica: Savacou Publications, 1989.

―――. "Shar. Hurricane Poem." *Caribana* 2 (1991): 14-23. Roma: Bulzoni, 1991.

_____. *Soweto*. Mona, Jamaica: Savacou Cooperative, 1979.

_____. *The Arrivants, A New World Trilogy, Rights of Passage* (1967), *Masks* (1968), Islands (1969). London: OUP, 1973.

_____. "The Love Axe/1: (Developing a Caribbean Aesthetic 1962-1974). Part One." (1977) *BIM* 16.61 (June 1977): 53-65.

_____. "The Love Axe/L: (Developing a Caribbean Aesthetic 1962-1974). Part Two." (1977) *BIM* 16.62 (Dec. 1977): 100-106.

_____. *The Namsetoura Papers*. http://tomraworth.com/np.pdf.

_____. *The Zea Mexican Diary*, 7 Sept. 1926 – 7 Sept. 1986. Madison, WI: The University of Wisconsin Press, 1993.

_____. *Third World Poems*. Harlow, Essex: Longman, 1983.

_____. *Word MakingMan*. Mona, Jamaica: Savacou Cooperative, 1979.

_____. *Words Need Love Too*. St. Martin: House of Nehesi Publishers, 2000.

_____. *X/Self*. New York: Oxford University Press, 1987.

Breiner, Laurence A. *An Introduction to West Indian Poetry*. Cambridge: Cambridge University Press, 1998.

Brother Resistance (Lutalo Makossa Masimba). *Rapso Explosion*. London: Karia Press. 1986.

Brown, John, ed. "Foreword." *Poems and Stories of St. Christopher, Nevis and Anguilla*. Basseterre, St. Kitts: U.C.W.I., 1960.

Brown, Stewart, ed. *Caribbean Poetry Now*. An Anthology. Foreword by Mervyn Morris, illustrated by Jennifer Northway. London: Hodder and Stoughton, 1986. 2nd ed. London: Edward Arnold, 1992.

_____, and Ian McDonald, eds. *The Heinemann Book of Caribbean Poetry*. London: Heinemann International Literature and Textbooks, 1992.

Bute, Ruby. *Golden Voices of S'maatin*. Philipsburg: House of Nehesi, 1989.

Carpentier, Alejo. *Crónicas Caribeñas*. Selección y prólogo Emilio Jorge Rodríguez. Biblioteca Alejo Carpentier, Documentos. La Habana, Cuba: Editorial Letras Cubanas, 2012.

Carter, Martin. *Poems of Affinity, 1978-1980*. Intr. Bill Carr; with an appreciation by Stanley Greaves. Georgetown, Guyana: Release Publishers, 1980.

_____. *Poems of Succession*. London; Port of Spain: New Beacon Books, 1977.

_____. *Selected Poems*. Georgetown, Guyana: Demerara, 1989.

_____. "The Location of the Artist." (1979) *University of Hunger, Collected Poems & Selected Prose*. Ed. Gemma Robinson. Highgreen, Northumberland: Bloodaxe Books, 2006. 232-234.

Cassidy, Frederic Gomes. *Jamaica Talk, Three Hundred Years of the English Language in Jamaica*. University of the West Indies Press: Kingston, 2007.

_____, and Robert Brock Le Page. *Dictionary of Jamaican English*. Cambridge: Cambridge University Press, 1967; 1980.

Césaire, Aimé. *Discourse on Colonialism*. New York: Monthly Review Press, 1972. Or. title *Discours sur le Colonialisme*. 1ère éd., Paris: Éditions Réclame, 1950; rééd. Paris: Présence Africaine Éditions, 1955; Paris, Présence Africaine Éditions, 1989.

Chamberlin, J. Edward. *Come Back to Me My Language, Poetry and the West Indies*. Chicago: University of Illinois Press, 1993.

Clarke, LeRoy. *De Distance Is Here. The El Tucuche Poems 1984-2007*. T&T: Ka.Ra.Da.Ele.Pa.Aye.Ada. 2007.

_____. "Interview with LeRoy Clarke." Ed. Tony Hall. *banyan*. Mt. Aripo, Trinidad: August 1985. 25 July 2008. http://www.pancaribbean.com/banyan/leroy.htm.

_____. "Interview with LeRoy Clarke." Ed. Maya Trotz. *Jouvay.com* (Feb. 2004) 25 July 2008 http://www.jouvay.com/interviews/leroyclarke.html.

_____. "LeRoy Clarke." The Art Society of Trinidad and Tobago 25 July 2008. http://artsocietytt.org/clarkeL.htm.

_____. "Voice of a Smouldering Coal…" 10 July 2009. Article sent by the poet. E-mail. 4 Nov. 2009.

Collins, Merle. *Because the Dawn Breaks! Poems dedicated to the Grenadian People*. London: Karia Press. 1985.

_____. *Lady in a Boat*. Leeds: Peepal Tree, 2003.

_____. *Rotten Pomerack*. London: Virago, 1992.

Condé, Maryse, ed. *La poésie antillaise*. Paris: Editions Fernand Nathan, 1977.

Cooke, Mel. "A poem per square mile." *Jamaica Gleaner* 20 Oct. 2005. http://www.jamaica-gleaner.com/gleaner/20051020/ent/ent1.html.

_____. "Salt of the earth finds voice." *Jamaica Gleaner* 17 Mar. 2006. http://www.jamaica-gleaner.com/gleaner/20060317/ent/ent4.html.

Dathorne, O.R., ed. *Caribbean Verse, An Anthology*. London: Heinemann, 1967.

Debien, Gabriel. "Le marronage." *Les esclaves aux Antilles françaises : XVIIe-XVIIIe siècles*. Basse-Terre: Societé d'histoire de la Guadeloupe; Fort-de-France: Societé d'histoire de la Martinique, 1974.

Donatien-Yssa, Patricia. "Leroy Clarke: The Double Ritual of Poetic and Plastic Creation, a Way to Freedom / Leroy Clarke entre Poésie et Peinture, Chantre de la Spiritualité et de la Liberté." La *Revue LISA / LISA e-journal* V.2 (2007) : 85. 4 May 2009 http://www.unicaen.fr/mrsh/lisa/publications/015/05Donatien-Yssa.pdf.

Eco, Umberto. *I limiti dell'interpretazione*. Milano: Bompiani, 1990.

Fergus, Howard A. *Love Labor Liberation in Lasana Sekou*. St. Martin: House of Nehesi Publishers, 2007.

Figueroa, John J.M., ed. *Caribbean Voices: An Anthology of West Indian Poetry, Volume 1, Dreams and Visions* (1966; 1968); *Volume 2, The Blue Horizons* (1970). Liverpool and Prescot: Evans Brothers Limited. 2 vols. 1966; 1968. 1970.

Fiorani, Flavio, e Marcello Flores. *Storia Illustrata dei Grandi Imperi Coloniali*. Milano: Giunti, 2005.

Florian, Sara. "Introduction." in Nicolaas, Quito. *Argus*. Amsterdam: In de Knipscheer. Forthcoming.

_____. "Looking for St. Maarten's 'Passion' in the *Pelican Heart* of Lasana Sekou." *Bajan Reporter* 23 Aug. 2011. http://www.bajanreporter.com/2011/08/looking-for-st-maartens-passion-in-the-pelican-heart-of-lasana-sekou-by-dr-sara-florian/.

_____. "Recensione a Edward Kamau Brathwaite, *Born to Slow Horses*, Middletown, Connecticut, WesleyanUniversity Press, 2005." *Il Tolomeo*, Articoli, *Recensioni e Inediti delle Nuove Letterature*. 10.1. Venezia: Studio LT2, 2007. 45-47.

_____. "Review of Earl McKenzie's *Palmer's Dream and Other Stories*." *The Sunday Observer*. Sunday 22nd July 2018. 4.

_____. "Review of Edward Kamau Brathwaite's Born to Slow Horses." *CQ. Caribbean Quarterly*. 55.1 (March 2009): 102-105. Kingston, Jamaica: University of the West Indies.

_____. Review of Lasana M. Sekou's *The Book of the Dead*. *Tripwire: a journal of poetics*, Buuck, David, Ed., Oakland, California: Bookmobile, 2019. 15. pp. 319-322.

_____. "The salt metaphor in St. Martin's literature; history as bane and bountiful reservoir of victories." Personal interview. Ed. Sara Florian. 15 May 2008. Philipsburg, St. Maarten.

Houseofnehesipublish.com. 12 Dec. 2009 http://www.houseofnehesipublish.com/interviews.html.

_____. "The quest for roots: Sekou's *Brotherhood of the Spurs* and the search for a St. Martin identity." *Moko magazine*. Issue 14. November 2018. http://mokomagazine.org/wordpress/the-quest-for-roots-sekous-brotherhood-of-the-spurs-and-the-search-for-a-st-martin-identity/.

Gadsby, Meredith. *Sucking Salt: Caribbean Women Writers, Migration, and Survival.* Columbia, Missouri: The University of Missouri Press, 2006.

Girvan, Norman. "Caribbean integration: can cultural production succeed where politics and economics have failed? (Confessions of a Wayward Economist)." "Presentation at a Colloquium on 'The Caribbean That Unites Us' in Santiago de Cuba, 5 July 2012. Revised version of St Martin Book Fair Presentation by the same name." http://www.normangirvan.info/wp-content/uploads/2012/07/santiago-paper.pdf. Posted on 15 Jul. 2012. Norman Girvan. Caribbean Political Economy. Wordpress. http://www.normangirvan.info/girvan-culture-in-tegration-confessions/.

Glissant, Édouard. *Caribbean Discourse, Selected Essays*. Trans. and with an introduction by J. Michael Dash. Charlottesville: UP of Virginia, 1989.

_____. *Caribbean Discourse. Selected Essays.* Trans. Ed. J. Michael Dash. Charlottesville: UP of Virginia, 1989. Or. publ. *Le Discours Antillais.* Paris: Éditions du Seuil, 1981.

Guillén, Nicolás. *New Love Poetry. Nueva Poesìa de Amor. En Algùn Sitio de la Primavera: Elegìa. In Some Springtime Place: Elegy.* Trans. Keith Ellis. Toronto; Buffalo; London: University of Toronto Press. 1994.

Hanna, Mary. "Sekou writes with 'erotic power'." *Jamaica Gleaner* 5 Nov. 2006. http:// www.jamaica-gleaner.com/gleaner/20061105/arts/arts4.html.

Hippolyte, Kendel. *Bearings*. <S.l.: s.n.>, 1986.

_____. *Birthright*. Leeds: Peepal Tree Press, 1997.

_____. *Confluences: Nine S. Lucian Poets*. Ed. Kendel Hippolyte. Castries, St. Lucia: The Source, 1988.

_____. *Island in the Sun, Side Two.... The Morne*, St. Lucia: Iouanalao Series No. 4, UWI Extra-Mural Dept. Iouanalao, 1980.

_____. *Night Vision*. Evanston, Illinois: TriQuarterly Books, Northwestern U.P., 2005.

_____. *The Labyrinth*. Castries, St. Lucia: The Source. 1993.

_____, and John Robert Lee, eds. *Saint Lucian Literature and Theatre. An Anthology of Reviews*. Castries, Saint Lucia: Cultural development Foundation. 2006.

Houat, Louis Timagène. *Les marrons*. Paris: Ebrard, 1844. rééd. By Metinger, Serge, and J.C. Carpanin. Océan Indien: Madagascar, La Réunion, Maurice. Paris: Omnibus, 1998.

Hutchinson, Joan Andrea. *Inna Mi Heart. Jamaican Love Poetry*. Kingston, Jamaica: Joan Andrea Hutchinson. 2007.

_____. *Meck Mi Tell Yuh*. Kingston, Jamaica: Joan Andrea Hutchinson. 2004.

_____. *Wild About Jamaica*. CD-ROM. Kingston, Jamaica: Joan Andrea Hutchinson. 2003.

Jack, Deborah Drisana. "Unhearting Memories: A Conversation with St. Martin Artist Deborah Jack." Ed. Jacqueline Bishop. *Calabash: A Journal of Caribbean Arts and Letters* 2.2 (Summer-Fall 2003): 87-107. eds. Jacqueline Bishop, and Michela Calderaro. New York: New York University. 19 Sept. 2009 http://www.nyu.edu/calabash/.

Joyette, Anthony. *Vincentian Poets, 1950 to 1980*. St. Laurent, Quebec: A F O, 1990.

Keane, Shake. *One a Week with Water: Rhymes and Notes*. Habana: Casa de las Américas, 1979.

_____. "Osmosis." *BIM* IV.15 (1951): 198.

_____. E. McG. "Some Religious Attitudes in W.I. Poetry. The Orthodox Attitude and Variations." *BIM* 4.15 (1952): 169-174.

_____. E. McG. "Some Religious Attitudes in W.I. Poetry. Nature and Religion." *BIM* 4.16 (1953): 266-271.

_____. *The Angel Horn—Collected Poems (1927-1997)*. St. Martin: House of Nehesi Publishers, 2005.

Knight, Franklin W. *The Caribbean, The Genesis of a Fragmented Nationalism*. New York: Oxford University Press, 1978.

Kobbe, Montague. "The Prose of Diction: Lasana Sekou's Short Stories." *The Weekender*, supplement of *The Daily Herald* (St. Maarten), 29 Nov. 2009. http://mtmkobbe.blogspot.sg/2009/11/prose-of-diction-lasana-sekous-short.html.

Kristeva, Julia. *La Rivoluzione del Linguaggio Poetico*. Venezia: Saggi Marsilio, 1979.

Lamming, George. *Coming, Coming Home—Conversations II: Western Education and the Caribbean Intellectual*. St. Martin: House of Nehesi Publishers. 1995; 2000.

_____. *In the Castle of my Skin*. London: Longman Caribbean Writers, 1998.

_____. "Myths in the Caribbean." *Anales del Caribe* (2003) Online version of the literary journal. La Habana, Cuba: Casa de las Américas. http://www.casadelasamericas.com/revistanales/2003/2003lamming.htm.

Lampe, Armando. "Por la aparición de *Double Play*," *Revista Mexicana del Caribe*, Vol. V, Núm. 010, 2000, Universidad de Quintana Roo, México. RMC, 10 (2000), 233-240.

Lang, George. *Entwisted Tongues, Comparative Creole Literatures*. Amsterdam & Atlanta: Rodopi, 2000.

Lee, John Robert, ed. *Roseau Valley and other Poems for Brother George Odlum, An Anthology*. Castries, St. Lucia: Jubilee Trust Fund, 2003.

Lewis, Sir Arthur. "On Being Different. The Graduation Address delivered at the U.W.I., Cave Hill, Barbados, on 5th February, 1971." (1971) BIM 14.53 (July-Dec. 1971): 3-9

McKenzie, Earl. "A Philosopher Who Also Writes and Paints." *Calabash: A Journal of Caribbean Arts and Letters* 4.2 (Spring/Summer 2007): 124-127. eds. Jacqueline Bishop, and Michela Calderaro. New York: New York University. 6 Jan. 2008 http://www.nyu.edu/calabash/.

Menkman, W.R. *De Nederlanders in het Caraibische Zeegebied waarin vervat de Geschiedenis der Nederlandsche Antillen*. P.N. Van Kampen & Zoon N.V.: Amsterdam, 1942.

Métraux, Alfred. *Voodoo*. Trans. Hugo Charteris. London: André Deutsch, 1959.

MiVi associates. "Sint Maarten / Saint Martin - 10-10-10: New Country in the Dutch Kingdom." *Lifestyle – Caribbean…the Caribbean at your fingertips* 6 Jul. 2012. http://www.lifestyle-caribbean.com/newstatusforstmaarten.html.

Morpeau, Louis. "La Muse Haïtienne d'Expression Créole." *Anthologie d'un siècle de poésie haïtienne 1817-1925*. Préface M. Fortunat Strowski. Paris: Bossard, 1925.

Nettleford, Rex. "The Caribbean's Creative Diversity: the Defining Point of the Region's History." Lecture delivered by Prof. Rex Nettleford, Vice Chancellor, University of the West Indies. University of Guyana, Guyana. 21 Mar. 2003. Press Release 54/2003. 4 April 2003.

Nowak, Mark. "Labor Love." 7 Feb. 2008. *Harriet*, A Blog from the Poetry Foundation. Posted by Angelo Rombley. 4 July 2008. 28 July 2008. http://www.poetryfoundation.org/harriet/2008/07/labor_love.html.

Omowale Maxwell, Marina. *About Our Own Business*. Arima, Trinidad: Drum Mountain Publications,1981. peepaltreepress. com. The best in Caribbean writing. 8 July 2008. http://www.peepaltreepress.com/author_display.asp?au_id=48.

Perosa, Sergio. *L'Isola, la Donna, il Ritratto*. Quattro Variazioni. Torino: Bollati Boringhieri, 1996.

Perse, St.-John. *Poésie/On Poetry. Speech of Acceptance upon the Award of the Nobel Prize for Literature*. Delivered in Stockholm December, 10, 1960. Trans. W. H. Auden. New York: Bollingen Foundation, 1961.

Pollard, Velma. *Dread Talk: the Language of Rastafari*. Montreal & Kingston: McGill-Queen's University Press, 2000.

Price, Richard and Sally. "Bookshelf 2005/2006 – *37 Poems*." Bookshelf 2005/2006: *New West Indian Guide / Nieuwe West-Indische*, 85-99. http://www.kitlv-journals.nl/index.php/nwig/article/viewFile/3589/4350.

Ramchand, Kenneth. *West Indian Poetry, An Anthology for Schools*. Kingston, Jamaica; San Juan, Trinidad: Longman Caribbean. 1971; 1989. 2nd ed.

Ramcharitar, Raymond. "CLR James—Celebrating CLR Three-day Conference Begins Today." *Express* (Trinidad). 20 Sept. 2001: 23.

Ramos, Abraham. "The Carib Sailors." BellyFull e-Newsletter. the Jewel's poetic vibez. New Anthology of Poetry. 2005. 30 June 2009. http://www.freewebs.com/bellyfull/november 2006.htm.

Ramos-Daly, Adele. "Chülühadiwa (We've Arrived)." *Black Orchid*. WAPS. Belize Writers and Poets Society. Founded 2007. 4 Aug. 2009. http://www.belizeanwaps.org/html/index.php?action=view&id=12&module=poemmodule&src=%40random48b32681f0ba4.

_____. "Poets Healing Belize." *Black Orchid*. In Belizean Poets Society. Lyrically Inspiring Belize. 2005. 31 May 2009 http://www.freewebs.com/belizeanpoetssociety /poetry.htm.

Roach, Eric M. *The Flowering Rock: Collected Poems 1938-1974*. Leeds: Peepal Tree Books, 1992.

Rochmann, Marie-Christine. *L'esclave fugitif dans la littérature antillaise*. Paris: Karthala, 2000.

Rodríguez, Emilio Jorge. *El Caribe Literario. Trazados de convivencia*. La Habana, Cuba: Editorial Arte y Literatura, 2011.

Rohlehr, F. Gordon. "Blues for Eric Roach." *My Strangled City and Other Essays*. Port of Spain, Trinidad: Longman Trinidad Limited. 1992. 142-3. First published in *Tapia* 4.21 (26 May 1974).

_____. "Blues and Rebellion: Edward Brathwaite's Rights of Passage." (1978) Ed. Emily Allen Williams. *The Critical Response to Kamau Brathwaite*. Westport, Connecticut; London: Praeger, 2004. 4-14.

_____. "Calypso, Literature and West Indian Cricket: Era of Dominance." *Anthurium – A Caribbean Studies Journal* 6.1 (Spring 2008) 30 July 2009 http://anthurium.miami.edu/volume_6/issue_1/rohlehr-calypso.html. Or. publ. "Transgression, Transition, Transformation: Essays in Caribbean Culture." San Juan, Trinidad: Lexington Trinidad Ltd, 2007.

_____. *Calypso & Society in Pre-Independence Trinidad*. Port of Spain, Trinidad: Lexicon Trinidad Ltd. 1990.

_____. *My Strangled City and Other Essays*. Port of Spain, Trinidad: Longman Trinidad Limited. 1992.

_____. "Songs of the Skeleton: Edward Brathwaite's Black + Blues, Part Three." (1986) Ed. Emily Allen Williams. *The Critical Response to Kamau Brathwaite*. Westport, Connecticut; London: Praeger, 2004. 102-118.

_____. *The Shape of That Hurt and Other Essays*. Port of Spain, Trinidad: Longman Trinidad Limited. 1992.

_____. "West Indian Poetry: Some Problems of Assessment. Part One." *BIM* 14.54 (Jan-June 1972): 80-88.

_____. "West Indian Poetry: Some Problems of Assessment. Part Two." (1972) *BIM* 14.55 (July-Dec. 1972): 134-144.

Rudder, David. "David Rudder talks about his songwriting." Online video. Posted by caribbeanpride. YouTube. 28 Aug. 2007. 3 Nov. 2008 http://www.youtube.comwatchv=jXSewmOv7wE.

Rutgers, Wim. "Dutch Caribbean Literature." eds. Mariles Glaser, and Marion Pausch. *Caribbean Writers/Les Auteurs Caribéens, Between Orality & Writing/Entre l'Oralité et l'Écriture*. Amsterdam; Atlanta, GA: Rodopi, 1994. 185-191.

Salter, Veronica, ed. "Kamau Monograph." Spec. issue of *Caribbean Quarterly* (2002). Mona, Kingston, Jamaica: University of the West Indies.

_____, ed. "The Unity is Submarine. Monograph." Spec. issue of CQ, *Caribbean Quarterly* 55:1. Mona, Kingston, Jamaica: University of the West Indies, March 2009.

Sekou, Lasana M. "Interview with Lasana M. Sekou." Interview with Lasana M. Sekou. Ed. Sara Florian. 2009. *Il Tolomeo*, Articoli, *Recensioni e Inediti delle Nuove Letterature*. 12.2. Venezia: Studio LT2, 2009. 97-103.

_____. "Schoonheid maakt de dichter bedeesd/(Beauty makes the poet shy)." Interview with Lasana M. Sekou. Ed. Hans Vaders. 10 May 2008. *Amigoe.com* 28 July 2008 http://www.amigoe.com/cgi-bin/artikel/exec/view.cgi?archive=94&num=42147.

_____. "The Polyglot Pride of St. Martin": Interview with Lasana M. Sekou. Ed. Sara Florian. *sx salon. a small axe literary platform*. 15 May 2008. http://smallaxe.net/wordpress3/inter

views/2010/10/27/%E2%80%9Cthe-polyglot-pride-of-st-martin%E2%80%9D-an-interview-with-lasana-sekou/.

Shaw, Andrew E. "Kei Miller, *Kingdom of Empty Bellies*. (Coventry, England: Heaventree Press, 2005). and Lasana M. Sekou, *37 Poems*. (St. Martin: House of Nehesi Publishers, 2005)." Reviews. *Journal of West Indian Literature* 16.1 (Nov. 2007): 105-110. Eds. Mark McWatt, Victor L. Chang, Evelyn O'Callaghan, and Michael Bucknor. Mona, Jamaica: Dept. of Literatures in English, The University of the West Indies. 105-111.

Spitzer, Leo. *Etudes de Style, Précédé de Leo Spitzer et la Lecture Stylistique de Jean Starobinski*. Paris: Gallimard, 1970.

"The importance of salt," 1999. http://mygeologypage.ucdavis.edu/cowen/~gel115/salt.html; SI, Salt Institute, "Salt in European history," http://www.saltinstitute.org/Uses-benefits/Salt-in-history/Salt-in-modern-history/Europe, 2011; and "Salt works," http://www.saltworks.us/salt_ info/si_HistoryOfSalt.asp, 2011. 17th July 2012.

Taylor, Jeremy and Lee, Simon. "Warrior Art." *BWIA Caribbean Beat. The Magazine of the True Caribbean* 15 (Sept.-Oct. 1995): 50-56. Caribbean Beat: Archive (1992-2006) 5 May 2009 http://www.meppublishers.com/online/caribbean-beat/archive/index.php? pid=6001&id=cb15-1-50.

Thieme, John. *Postcolonial Con-texts: Writing Back to the Canon*. London & New York: Continuum, 2001.

Todorov, Tzvetan. "Esclavagisme, colonialisme et communication." *La Conquête de l'Amérique, La Question de l'Autre*. Paris: Seuil, 1982.

_____. I *Formalisti Russi, Teoria della Letteratura e Metodo Critico*. Trans. Gian Luigi Bravo. Torino: Einaudi, 1986. Or. title *Théorie de la littérature*.

Torres-Saillant, Silvio. *Caribbean Poetics, Toward an Aesthetic of West Indian Literature*. Cambridge: Cambridge University Press, 1997.

Unigwe, Chika. "*The Salt Reaper: Poems from the Flats.*" *Postcolonial Text*, Vol. 2 No.3 (2006). http://postocolonial.org/index.php/pct/article/viewFile/470/316.

Walcott, Derek. *Collected Poems 1948-1984*. London: Faber & Faber, 1986.

_____. "Derek Walcott in conversation with Kwame Dawes." Calabash Literary Festival. 24 May 2008. Treasure Beach, St. Elizabeth, Jamaica.

_____. "Society and the Artist." (1957). Ed. Robert Hamner. *Critical Perspectives on Derek Walcott*. Washington D.C.: Three Continents Press, 1993.

_____. *The Antilles: Fragments of Epic Memory*. London: Faber & Faber, 1993. Repr. *What the Twilight Says: Essays*. New York: Farrar, Straus and Giroux, 1998.

_____. *The Arkansas Testament*. New York: Farrar, 1987.

Ward, Rochelle. "Sekou's nine stories birthing a St. Martin nation – Discoveries and still more questions." *The Bajan Reporter* 9 Mar. 2010 http://bajanreporter.com/?p=8880.

Warner-Lewis, Maureen. "Language Use in West Indian Literature." *A History of Literature in the Caribbean. Vol. 2 English- and Dutch-speaking Regions*. Offprint, Amsterdam; Philadelphia: John Benjamins Publishing Company, 2001. 25-37.

_____. "The Rhythms of Caribbean Vocal and Oral-Based Texts." *Caribbean Culture: Soundings on Kamau Brathwaite*. Ed. Annie Paul. Kingston, Jamaica: University of the West Indies Press, 2007. 54-75.

White, Hayden. *Tropics of Discourse, Essays in Cultural Criticism*. London: The John Hopkins University Press, 1978.

About the Author

Sara Florian obtained a Ph.D. in Modern Philology at Cà Foscari University, Italy. She has studied at the Université La Sorbonne-Paris IV, the École Normale Supérieure in Paris, and the Summer School collaborative program of Harvard University and Cà Foscari University. Her postdoc in Contemporary Singapore Literature was obtained at Singapore Management University. Dr. Florian has studied Caribbean literature extensively at the research facilities of The University of the West Indies in Jamaica, Trinidad, and Barbados—where she interviewed noted authors and scholars such as Mutabaruka, Gordon Rohlehr, Kenneth Ramchand, Edward Baugh, Mervyn Morris, St Hope Earl McKenzie, Maureen Warner-Lewis, Carolyn Cooper, Jeannette Allsopp, Kendel Hippolyte, John Robert Lee, AJA, David Rudder, Hubert Devonish, Funso Aiyejina, Velma Pollard, Jean D'Costa, and Jennifer Rahim. Her comparative language and literature studies have also taken her to St. Martin, USA, and Australia. Dr. Florian teaches Italian at the National University of Singapore. According to Dr. Florian, "My infatuation with ancient history led me, as a side passion, to share Latin and ancient Greek with my students. My Venetian roots have accompanied me through various uprooting and re-routing journeys. Like the beautiful city on the water, I share an independent spirit of survival and intellectual curiosity, which steered me toward my first encounter with Caribbean literature." Dr. Florian loves painting and her literature reviews, essays, poems, and short stories have appeared in *Small Axe/sx salon*, *Tripwire*, *Caribbean Quarterly*, *The Sunday Observer*, *Moko – Caribbean Arts and Letters*, *The Sunday Gleaner*, and *The Jamaica Observer*. *Luce, la città morente che mi ha fatto rinascere / Light, the dying city which gave me life again* (2011) is her debut bilingual novel. Dr. Florian is among the new generation of Caribbeanist scholars, and *Caribbean Counterpoint: The Aesthetics of Salt in Lasana Sekou* is her first book on comparative and contemporary Caribbean literature.